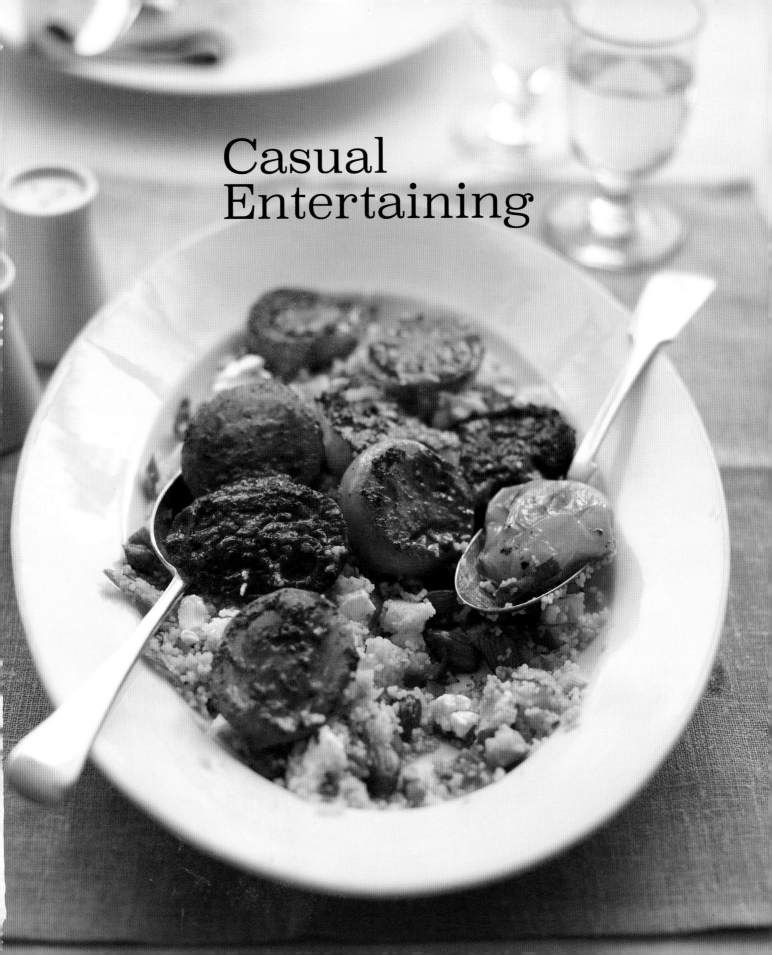

Casual Entertaining

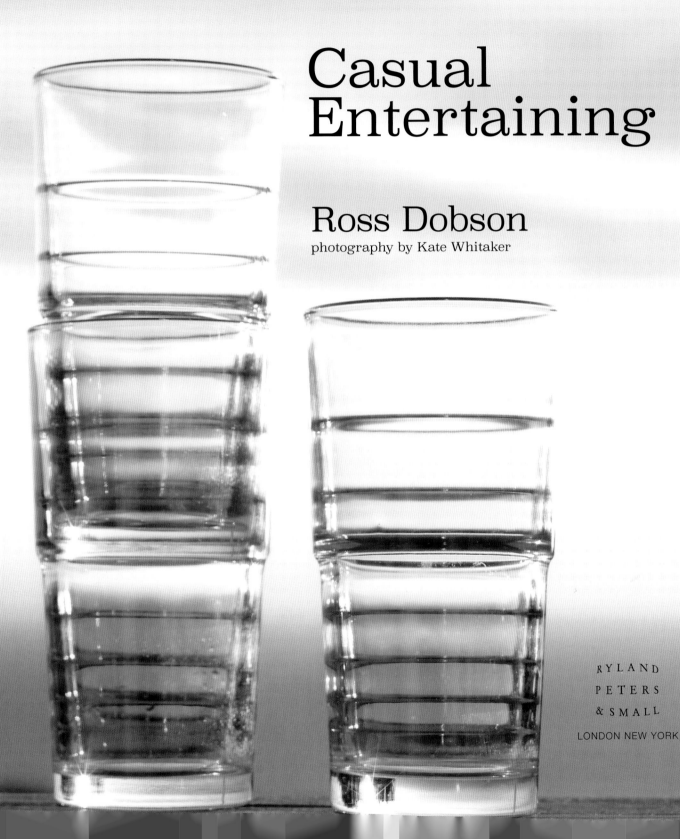

Casual
Entertaining

Ross Dobson

photography by Kate Whitaker

RYLAND
PETERS
& SMALL

LONDON NEW YORK

Dedication
For Matthew Lynch

Design and Photographic Art Direction
Steve Painter
Commissioning Editor Julia Charles
Production Toby Marshall
Publishing Director Alison Starling
Art Director Leslie Harrington

Food Stylist Ross Dobson
Prop Stylist Liz Belton
Indexer Hilary Bird

Author's Acknowledgements

Once again, a great big thank you to Alison for her confidence, support and the opportunity to do this lovely project. Thanks to Julia for again keeping me on my toes and being the best editor anyone could wish for. To my now old mate Steve – not sure if cocktail making is your forte, eh Steve? But you are a mighty fine designer nonetheless and a lot less worrisome these days... do hope I get to work with you again. The same goes for Kate – lovely photography my dear and you are a sheer joy to work with. Big thanks to Liz whose great choice of props made our lives much easier on the shoot and brings life to these pages. Thanks to Susan, photographer's assistant extraordinaire, who smiled even in winter on the howling cliffs of hell in Cornwall. And to Matt, for coming along for the short ride and keeping us entertained with your wonderful, positive energy.

First published in the United Kingdom
in 2009
by Ryland Peters & Small
20–21 Jockey's Fields
London WC1R 4BW
www.rylandpeters.com

10 9 8 7 6 5 4 3 2 1

Text © Ross Dobson 2009
Design and photographs
© Ryland Peters & Small 2009

ISBN: 978 1 84597 907 2

A catalogue record for this book
is available from the British Library.

Printed and bound in China.

Notes

- All spoon measurements are level unless otherwise specified.

- Eggs are medium unless otherwise specified. Uncooked or partially cooked eggs should not be served to the very old, frail, young children, pregnant women or those with compromised immune systems.

- When a recipe calls for the zest of lemons or limes, buy unwaxed fruit and wash well before using. If you can only find treated fruit, scrub well in warm, soapy water before using.

- Ovens should be preheated to the specified temperature. Recipes in this book were tested using a regular oven. If using a fan-assisted oven, follow the manufacturer's instructions for adjusting temperatures.

contents

keeping it casual

When I am entertaining at home I have a mantra – keep it simple and keep it casual. I just can't see the point of making food that keeps me away from my family and friends or costs a small fortune. After all, isn't sharing food and enjoying good company what entertaining is all about?

Thankfully, in recent years many of us have moved away from the traditional notions of entertaining – by which I mean strictly adhering to the rules of seating everyone around a dining table and serving up a fancy starter, a main course and a dessert. I can recall a time when any French dish was considered to be the epitome of style. What did a soufflé ever do but stress out the cook, and more often than not disappoint? As we have changed the way we cook and eat every day, entertaining at home has also become a far more relaxed and casual affair, and there is no longer pressure on the cook to slave over a hot stove for days. Of course, there is nothing to stop you from serving up a three-course dinner if that's what you want to do, but the heat is off and the choice is now yours.

This shift is largely because we have now been exposed to, and indeed have embraced, new foods and flavours along with new cooking and eating styles from all around the world. When planning my menus, I like to draw upon many influences. In particular, I have a deep respect and love of food from the southern Mediterranean countries – who has a more joyful and casual approach to entertaining than the Italians or the Spanish? The exotic flavours and simple cooking techniques of North Africa and the Middle East also make for easy work. I'm a big fan of slow-cooked Moroccan tagines and couscous salads packed with fresh herbs. And when speed is the issue, nothing beats a spicy stir-fried South East Asian noodle or rice recipe.

Also, now, more than ever before, we give more thought to where our food comes from and the quality of produce. Many of us enjoy spending time at farmers' markets and hand-picking our produce, making the process of cooking and eating it more meaningful and rewarding. You may even prefer to plan your entertaining ideas around your favourite produce or what looks good at the market on the day. This is a very different approach to that of days gone by when spending a large amount on ingredients and then sweating over multi-paged, complex recipes was the norm. It's hardly relaxing for guests to arrive only to find the host in a stressed-out mess and a kitchen turned upside down – it's enough to spoil anyone's appetite!

In my view, there are really three main types of recipe that work well when entertaining and the first is anything that can be prepared ahead of time – a dish that can be baked the day beforehand is a boon, especially if it actually tastes better the next day! The second type is a slow-cooked recipe, which, once assembled and popped in the oven, pretty much looks after itself, leaving the cook free to get on with other tasks. The third is a quick and easy recipe that is started from scratch but thrown together in less than 20 minutes – great for when time is short. If a recipe meets any one of these criteria, it's likely to be a great recipe for entertaining.

The time of year, the occasion, the amount of time you have available and the tastes of the people you are feeding will all dictate what you decide to cook. You'll find recipes here for almost every scenario, but they all have one thing in common – they will let you enjoy the company of your guests. In short, recipes that will take the fear out of entertaining and make you want to invite people to your home to eat more often.

Sharing plates are a part of most cuisines around the world – from Greek and Middle Eastern meze to Spanish tapas and North African kemia. This relaxed style of eating is about picking and grazing on a variety of small, tasty dishes and fingerfoods rather than ploughing through a substantial plate of food with a knife and fork. It's a great way to entertain friends for a few hours with drinks, instead of committing to an entire evening. In the Grazing chapter I've given you ideas for dishes that are ideal for sharing, along with recipes for drinks that pair well with them.

More often than not we just don't have the time (or stamina!) to spend several hours in the kitchen, especially after a long day at work. When you are pressed for time and low on energy, fast and fresh food is what's needed. In Food in a Flash you'll find recipes that fit the bill perfectly. Stock up on inexpensive storecupboard essentials that will make life easier. Spices and sauces will add depth of flavour to basic foods, and staples such as dried pasta, noodles and couscous will prove invaluable. All you need to do is combine these with a few fresh ingredients to produce tasty dishes.

When money is in short supply and it's time to tighten your belt, eating at home is by far the cheaper option than dining out at a restaurant. In Cheap and Cheerful I've included recipes that will allow you to feed your friends without blowing your budget. Make the most of the alchemy of slow-cooking and turn cheaper cuts of meat into delicious casseroles or embrace comfort food and make substantial veggie bakes that everyone will love.

There are of course occasions when you do want to treat yourself or others and that's where the recipes in Chic Eats come in. Even elegant eating doesn't mean you have to spend hours in the kitchen – the key is to buy the best fresh ingredients, such as a lovely piece of wild salmon or an organic chicken, cook it simply and serve with well-thought-out side dishes.

When I make something sweet for my guests (which is, to be honest, every time I have guests!) I like to work backwards, making the dessert first. I feel as if the world is all in order if the dessert is sitting in the refrigerator waiting to be served. So I've also included ideas for Sweet Things that are guaranteed to impress, whether it's a speedy cheat's mousse or an indulgent baked dessert that benefits from being made the day ahead.

grazing

spicy Cajun mixed nuts

I have given cashews, pecans and pistachios in the ingredient list here, but feel free to choose your favourite nuts for this. Buy the nuts in bulk and you will save heaps of cash. And besides, this is a recipe you will want to make more than once – whenever I have served this up with drinks it is not uncommon for me to be emailed the next day asking for that 'great nut recipe'. It's a good nibble to offer if you are planning to serve a more spicy meal later on.

155 g unsalted cashews
155 g pecans
140 g pistachios
1 teaspoon cayenne pepper
1 teaspoon smoked paprika (pimentón)
½ teaspoon dried thyme
1 teaspoon fine sea salt
1 tablespoon soft brown sugar
1 tablespoon olive oil

a baking tray lined with baking paper

Serves 10–12

Preheat the oven to 180°C (350°F) Gas 4.

Put all of the nuts in a large bowl. Add the cayenne pepper, paprika, thyme, salt and sugar and mix to combine. Stir in the olive oil. Tip the nuts out onto the prepared baking tray, spreading them out into a single layer.

Bake in the preheated oven for 10 minutes, stirring about halfway through the cooking time. Let cool completely before spooning into serving bowls. Perfect served with any of the drinks recipes given on this page, these nuts will keep in an airtight container for 7–10 days.

promello

125 ml ruby red grapefruit juice, chilled
1 bottle (750 ml) prosecco, chilled

Serves 6–8

Pour about 1 tablespoon of the grapefruit juice into a champagne glass and top up with prosecco. Serve immediately.

grown-up lemonade

125 ml freshly squeezed lemon juice
3 tablespoons caster sugar
2 lemons, thinly sliced
a handful of fresh mint leaves
125 ml white rum
750 ml soda water
ice cubes, to serve

Serves 6

Combine the lemon juice and sugar in a small saucepan. Cook over high heat until boiling, reduce the heat to medium and simmer for 4–5 minutes, until syrupy. Let cool.

Put the ice cubes, lemon slices, mint and rum in a large jug. Stir to combine and add the soda water. Serve immediately.

summer fruit punch

250 ml apple juice
250 ml low-sugar lemonade
2 peaches, stoned and roughly chopped
12 strawberries, to garnish
1 bottle (750 ml) champagne or any sparkling white wine, chilled
ice cubes, to serve

Serves 12

Combine the apple juice, lemonade and peaches in a bowl or large jug and refrigerate until chilled.

Put a few scoops of ice cubes in a serving jug or glasses with a strawberry to garnish. Add the apple juice mixture and top up with champagne. Serve immediately.

See photograph on pages 10–11.

Parmesan biscuits

This is a robust savoury biscuit made using an old catering trick that I'm very fond of – using clingfilm to roll the mixture into a log and then refrigerating it until needed. All you then have to do is cut the chilled dough into slices and bake. The inclusion of smoked paprika gives these a distinctly Spanish feel, making them great to serve with a wedge of manchego cheese and some Spanish quince paste (membrillo) on the side.

125 g unsalted butter, cubed and softened
80 g mature Cheddar cheese, grated
20 g Parmesan cheese, finely grated
150 g plain flour
¼ teaspoon smoked paprika (pimentón)

a baking tray lined with baking paper

Makes about 60

Combine the butter and both cheeses in a food processor. Add the flour and paprika and process until just combined and the mixture forms into lots of smaller balls of dough. Add 1–2 tablespoons cold water and process until the dough roughly comes together.

Lay a sheet of clingfilm on a work surface and spoon half of the mixture down the centre to form a log, about 3 cm across. Firmly roll up. Repeat with the remaining dough to make 2 logs and refrigerate for about 1 hour, until firm. Alternatively, keep in the freezer until needed.

Preheat the oven to 180ºC (350ºF) Gas 4.

Finely slice the log and arrange the discs on the prepared baking tray. Bake in the preheated oven for 8–10 minutes and then transfer to a wire rack to cool and become crisp. These will keep in an airtight container for 2 days or you can freeze the uncooked dough for up to 1 month.

minty Pimm's

250 ml Pimm's No 1
750 ml dry ginger ale
1 tablespoon freshly squeezed lime juice
1 small cucumber, thinly sliced
a handful of fresh mint leaves
ice cubes, to serve

Serves 4

Chill 4 serving glasses. Combine the Pimm's, ginger ale and lime juice in a jug. Put the cucumber, mint leaves and ice cubes into the serving glasses and add the Pimm's mixture. Serve immediately.

white sangria

1 bottle (750 ml) dry white wine
125 ml freshly squeezed orange juice
2 tablespoons caster sugar
2 oranges, peeled and white pith removed, thinly sliced
1 punnet strawberries, hulled and halved
125 ml dry gin
ice cubes, to serve

Serves 4–6

Put the white wine, orange juice, sugar, fruit and gin in a large jug and refrigerate for 3 hours, until well chilled, stirring often so that the sugar dissolves.

Put the ice cubes in a large serving jug and pour over the sangria. Serve immediately.

See photograph on pages 2–3.

polenta chips with green Tabasco mayonnaise

Don't we all just love something fried every now and then? Everything in moderation. I have cooked these chips in the past and made the mistake of 'testing' one or two beforehand. Be warned that it is hard to stop at just one!

1 litre chicken or vegetable stock
250 g instant polenta
25 g butter
50 g Parmesan cheese, finely grated
250 ml vegetable oil
125 ml light olive oil
30 g plain flour
125 ml mayonnaise
2 teaspoons green Tabasco sauce

2 baking trays, lightly oiled

Makes about 60

Put the stock in a saucepan and bring to the boil. While the stock is boiling, pour in the polenta in a steady stream and whisk until it is all incorporated. Continue whisking for about 2 minutes, until the mixture is smooth and thickened. Remove from the heat and stir through the butter and Parmesan until well combined. Spoon half of the mixture into each of the trays. Use the back of a metal spoon to smooth the top. Cover and refrigerate for at least 4 hours, until firm.

Transfer the polenta to a chopping board. Trim the edges. Cut the block lengthways in half – then cut into 1-cm thick slices, to make about 60 chips.

Pour the oils into a frying pan and heat over medium/high heat. The oil is ready if a small piece of the polenta mixture sizzles on contact. Put about one quarter of the chips in a colander and sprinkle over some of the flour. Shake the colander to coat the chips in the flour and to remove the excess. Add these to the oil and cook for 4–5 minutes, turning often, until golden. Transfer the cooked chips to some kitchen paper to absorb the excess oil. Cover with foil and keep warm in a low oven while you cook the second batch. Repeat with the other chips.

Combine the mayonnaise and Tabasco in a bowl to serve alongside the hot chips as a dip.

toasted mozzarella and basil fingers

These could define casual entertaining for me. I live near a local supplier of hand-made smoked mozzarella, which might be tricky for you to find. If you have trouble sourcing it, don't miss out; simply substitute buffalo mozzarella or even a strongly flavoured fontina. These cheesy snacks are great with beer or chilled white wine.

8 thin slices of white bread
200 g mozzarella cheese, preferably smoked
a large handful of shredded fresh basil leaves
4 tablespoons olive oil
sea salt and freshly ground black pepper

Makes 16–20

Trim any larger crusts off the bread without being too fussy. Lay 4 slices of the bread on a work surface and divide the cheese and basil on top. Add a slice of bread to each.

Preheat a large, non-stick frying pan over medium heat and add 2 tablespoons of the olive oil. Sit the sandwiches in the pan and drizzle the remaining oil on the top slices of bread.

Cook for 2–3 minutes, using a spatula to gently press down on the sandwiches. Turn over and cook for a further 2 minutes. Transfer to a chopping board and cut each sandwich into 4–5 thin fingers. Season with a little salt and pepper and serve immediately while the mozzarella is still molten.

Variation: For a spicy treat, try replacing the basil with a little smoked chilli jelly, available from gourmet retailers.

merguez sausages

Serve these homemade spicy sausages with some marinated olives and good crusty bread.

500 g beef mince
2 garlic cloves, crushed
2 teaspoons ground cumin
1 teaspoon ground coriander
1 teaspoon cayenne pepper
1 teaspoon sea salt
light olive oil, for brushing

spicy tomato sauce:
400-g tin whole plum tomatoes
1 red onion, chopped
1 large red chilli, chopped
1 teaspoon smoked paprika (pimentón)
1 tablespoon soft brown sugar
1 tablespoon olive oil

a baking tray lined with baking paper

Serves 4–6

Put the mince, garlic, spices and salt in a large bowl and use your hands to combine. Throw the mixture against the side of the bowl a few times. Cover with clingfilm and refrigerate for 1–2 hours.

To make the tomato sauce, preheat the oven to 180ºC (350ºF) Gas 4. Put the tomatoes (with their juice), onion, chilli, paprika, sugar and olive oil in a roasting tin. Stir to combine and cook in the preheated oven for 1 hour, stirring often. Transfer to a food processor and blend until smooth.

Using wet hands, take about 1 heaped tablespoon of the mince, roll it into a small sausage (about 5–6 cm long) and put it on the prepared baking tray. Repeat until you have used all of the mixture. Preheat the grill to high. Lightly brush the sausages with oil and cook for about 6–8 minutes, turning, until brown. Serve with the sauce.

filo 'cigars' with halloumi

Fried in a little oil, filo pastry cooks to a lovely golden crisp. These 'cigars' freeze well (laid between sheets of baking paper) and can be cooked from frozen, making them perfect for parties or impromptu drinks.

4 sheets of filo pastry, defrosted if frozen
200 g halloumi cheese, grated
50 g feta cheese, grated
125 g butter, melted and cooled
80 g stoned and sliced black olives
16 small fresh mint leaves
light olive oil, for frying

a baking tray lined with baking paper

Makes 16

Cut each sheet of filo in half lengthways. Stack them on top of each other, then cover with a large piece of baking paper. Place a damp tea towel on top of the paper to prevent the filo from drying out.

Combine the halloumi and feta in a bowl. Lay a sheet of filo on a clean work surface with one of the short ends nearest to you. Lightly brush all over with melted butter. Spoon 1 tablespoon of the cheese mixture on the end of the filo, about 1–2 cm from the edge, and use your fingers to mould it into a small log. Top with 2–3 slices of olive and a few mint leaves. Roll over the edge nearest to you to enclose the filling, then fold in the sides. Brush the folded-down sides with a little butter, then roll up quite tightly to form a small, cigar-shaped parcel. Repeat to make 16, putting them on the prepared baking tray as you go.

Set a frying pan over high heat and brush with a little oil. Cook the 'cigars' for 2–3 minutes, turning often until they are golden and crisp. Serve warm.

roast pumpkin, feta and olive empanadas

Argentinian empanadas are often filled with spiced meat, but here is a delicious vegetarian version.

500 g peeled, deseeded and roughly chopped pumpkin
1 red onion, chopped
2 garlic cloves, roughly chopped
½ teaspoon cumin seeds
2 tablespoons olive oil
2 teaspoons white wine vinegar
3 sheets of ready-rolled puff pastry, defrosted if frozen
60 g feta cheese, grated
1 tablespoon milk

a baking tray lined with baking paper
a biscuit cutter, about 12 cm diameter

Makes 12

To make the filling, preheat the oven to 220ºC (425ºF) Gas 7. Combine the pumpkin, onion, garlic, cumin and oil in a small baking dish. Add the vinegar and 65 ml water and cook in the oven for about 30 minutes, until the pumpkin is tender and golden and the liquid has evaporated. Transfer to a bowl, roughly mash with a fork and season to taste. Let cool until needed.

Preheat the oven to 220ºC (425ºF) Gas 7. Unroll the pastry and lay it on a clean work surface. Use the biscuit cutter to stamp out 12 circles. Put 1 tablespoon of filling in the centre of each circle and top with a little crumbled feta. Brush cold water around the edge of each one just to moisten and fold over to form a half-moon shape. Pinch the edges between your thumb and index finger to seal. Put on the prepared baking tray. Brush the top of each with milk. Bake in the preheated oven for about 20 minutes, until lightly golden. Serve warm.

garlic-infused olive oil, warm marinated olives and jamón serrano platter

This sharing plate is simplicity itself to put together and absolutely no preparation is needed once your guests arrive. Lay out the platter and let it sit at room temperature for a short while before serving and have the all-important bevvie ready too. A fruity sangria such as the one on page 14 would be perfect.

garlic-infused olive oil:
8 garlic cloves, unpeeled
65 ml light olive oil
65 ml extra virgin olive oil
2 tablespoons balsamic vinegar

warm marinated olives:
100 g large green olives, such as Sicilian
100 g small black olives, such as Ligurian
250 ml extra virgin olive oil
2 sprigs of fresh thyme
2 dried red chillies
1 bay leaf
2 thin slices of orange peel

8 slices of jamón serrano (Spanish salted, air-dried ham)
good crusty bread, to serve

Serves 6–8

To make the garlic-infused olive oil, put the garlic cloves and light olive oil in a small saucepan and cook over medium heat for 5 minutes. Remove from the heat and let cool. Add the extra virgin olive oil and vinegar and transfer to a serving bowl.

Put the olives in a small, heatproof bowl. Put the oil, thyme, chillies, bay leaf and orange peel in a small saucepan. Set over medium heat. As soon as you hear the herbs starting to sizzle in the oil, remove the pan from the heat and pour the mixture over the olives. Let cool for 20 minutes.

To serve, arrange the still-warm garlic-infused oil, olives, jamón and bread on a platter and let your guests help themselves.

slow-cooked tomatoes with goat's cheese and garlic toasts

It might seem that oven-roasted tomatoes have been done to death in the last few years – so much so that it's easy to forget just how good they are when done well! This is a very slow-cooked version, almost like a confit. Do use in-season tomatoes for a sweet, heady flavour that works well with the tart goat's cheese.

500 ml extra virgin olive oil
1 sprig of fresh oregano
2 teaspoons finely chopped fresh flat leaf parsley leaves
6 very ripe Roma tomatoes
½ teaspoon sea salt
200 g soft goat's cheese
1 small baguette
2 garlic cloves, peeled

Serves 4

Preheat the oven to 130°C (250°F) Gas ½.

Put the oil in a small, non-reactive baking dish. Add the oregano and parsley. Cut the tomatoes in half and arrange them in a single layer in the dish. Ideally you want the tomatoes to be almost fully submerged in the oil. Sprinkle the salt evenly over the tomatoes. Cook in the preheated oven for about 5 hours, until the tomatoes are intensely red and softened yet still retain their shape. Remove from the oven and leave the tomatoes in the oil to cool completely.

Put the goat's cheese in a serving bowl.

Preheat the grill. Slice the baguette very thinly. Toast the bread on both sides until golden and crisp and rub one side with the peeled garlic cloves.

Remove the tomatoes from the oil and arrange them on a serving platter with the cheese and garlic toasts on the side.

See photograph on page 22.

roasted red pepper and walnut dip

This is a traditional Syrian dip called muhammara. There it would be served as part of a meze selection, with houmous, aubergine dip (baba ganoush), pickles, olives, cheese and flatbreads. It also works well as a spooning sauce to serve with baked or grilled fish or lamb. It's perfect for entertaining, as it benefits from being made a day in advance.

3 large red peppers
1 slice of day-old sourdough bread, cut into small pieces
100 g walnut halves, coarsely chopped
½ teaspoon dried chilli flakes
1 tablespoon sun-dried tomato paste
2 garlic cloves, chopped
2 teaspoons freshly squeezed lemon juice
1 tablespoon balsamic vinegar
2 teaspoons caster sugar
1 teaspoon ground cumin
2 tablespoons olive oil, plus extra to serve
chopped pistachios, to sprinkle
sea salt and freshly ground black pepper
toasted flatbread, roughly torn, to serve

Serves 6–8

Cook the peppers one at a time by skewering each one on a fork and holding it directly over a gas flame for 10–15 minutes, until the skin is blackened all over. Alternatively, put them on a baking tray and then in an oven preheated to 220°C (425°F) Gas 7. Cook them for about 10–15 minutes, until the skin has puffed up and blackened all over. Transfer to a bowl, cover with a tea towel and leave until cool enough to handle.

Using your hands, remove the skin and seeds from the peppers and tear the flesh into pieces. (Avoid rinsing with water, as this will remove the smoky flavour.) Put it in a food processor and add the remaining ingredients. Process to a coarse paste. Season to taste with salt and pepper and transfer to a bowl. Cover with clingfilm and refrigerate for at least 8 hours to allow the flavours to develop.

To serve, bring the dip to room temperature and transfer it to a shallow bowl. Drizzle with olive oil and sprinkle with chopped pistachios. Serve with torn toasted flatbreads. It will keep in an airtight container in the refrigerator for 4–5 days.

See photograph on page 23.

sesame prawn toasts with pickled carrot

When entertaining it helps if you think of yourself as a caterer and use some tricks of the trade. Dishes that can be made ahead of time are very useful – the prawn mixture here can be 'prepped' several hours in advance and the toasts simply cooked to order.

300 g raw peeled and deveined prawns
6 spring onions, finely chopped
1 tablespoon finely grated fresh ginger
2 teaspoons dry sherry (optional)
1 teaspoon light soy sauce
1 egg white, lightly beaten
6 thick slices of white bread
50 g sesame seeds
sea salt
about 250 ml vegetable oil, for shallow frying
sprigs of fresh coriander, to garnish

pickled carrot:
1 large carrot, coarsely grated
2 tablespoons Japanese pickled ginger, sliced
2 tablespoons juice from the pickled ginger jar
½ teaspoon caster sugar
2 shallots, thinly sliced on the diagonal

Makes 24 toasts

To make the pickled carrot, combine the carrot, pickled ginger, pickled ginger juice, sugar and shallots in a small, non-reactive bowl. Set aside until needed.

Put the prawns, spring onions, ginger, sherry, soy sauce, egg white and some salt in a food processor. Process until roughly chopped.

Trim the crusts off the bread and discard or save for another use. Cut each slice into 4 triangles. Put the sesame seeds on a plate. Spread about 2 teaspoons of the prawn mixture onto each piece of bread, pressing down lightly. Press each triangle into the sesame seeds to lightly coat.

Put the oil in a shallow frying pan and heat over medium/high heat. Add a piece of bread to test if the oil is ready – if the bread sizzles on contact, the oil is hot enough. Use a fish slice to carefully add the prawn toasts to the pan, prawn-side down, and cook for 1 minute. Turn over and cook for 1 minute more, until golden. Drain on kitchen paper. Spoon a little pickled carrot over the top of each toast and add a sprig of coriander. Serve immediately.

chilli salt squid

We really ought to eat more squid; it is cheap and in plentiful supply. Fresh squid can look a little scary, but it really is superior to the frozen stuff. It should be cooked in one of two ways: very quickly or for a long time – anywhere in between makes it tough.

400 g cleaned squid (1 large tube)
2 tablespoons cornflour
1 tablespoon plain flour
½ teaspoon ground white pepper
½ teaspoon mild chilli powder
3 teaspoons sea salt
1 large red chilli, thinly sliced
a small handful of fresh coriander leaves, chopped
vegetable oil, for deep-frying
lemon wedges, to serve

Serves 4

Cut the squid tube down one side so that it opens up. Use a sharp knife to trim and discard any internal membranes. Cut it lengthways into 2-cm wide strips, then cut each strip in half. Combine the flours, pepper, chilli powder and salt in a large bowl. Half-fill a saucepan with the vegetable oil and heat over high heat until the surface of the oil shimmers.

Toss half of the squid pieces in the flour mixture, quickly shaking off the excess, and add them to the oil. Cook for about 2 minutes, until deep golden. Remove with a slotted spoon and drain on kitchen paper. Repeat with the remaining squid. Add the chilli slices to the oil and cook for just a few seconds. Remove from the pan and drain on kitchen paper. Put the squid and chilli on a serving plate and sprinkle with the coriander. Serve while still warm with plenty of lemon wedges on the side for squeezing.

grown-up fish fingers

This recipe is one of the more elegant in this chapter but it's still very casual. Good-quality ingredients are the key here – kingfish is a variety of fish local to me, so ask your fishmonger for other suggestions if you can't find it. Tuna, marlin or mahi-mahi would work.

200 g kingfish fillet or any firm sashimi-grade fish
2 tablespoons extra virgin olive oil
2 tablespoons freshly squeezed lemon juice
3 thick of slices sourdough bread
2 tablespoons unsalted butter, softened
2 shallots, very thinly sliced
a handful of fresh flat leaf parsley leaves, roughly chopped
sea salt and freshly ground black pepper

Serves 4

Put the fish in a non-reactive bowl with 1 tablespoon of the oil and 1 tablespoon of the lemon juice. Toss to coat, cover and set aside for 10 minutes.

Set a non-stick frying pan over high heat. Season the fish well with salt and pepper, add it to the pan and cook for 1 minute. Turn over and cook for 1 minute more. Transfer to a plate and let cool.

Toast the bread on both sides, until very golden and the crusts are almost starting to burn. Spread liberally with butter on one side and trim off the crusts. Cut the toast lengthways in half, then across in half to give 12 'fingers'.

Using a sharp knife, cut the fish crossways into 12 even slices and put a piece on the buttered side of each toasted finger.

Whisk the remaining oil and lemon juice in a small, non-reactive bowl. Top each finger with a small mound of shallot, spoon over some dressing and sprinkle over the parsley. Season with salt and pepper and serve immediately.

two savoury palmiers

Here are two variations on the classic crumbly puff pastry biscuit – both are delicious served with drinks. The extreme savouriness of both miso and Parmesan makes them a good flavour match. The onion jam option is more classic – the jam itself sits nicely on an antipasti plate, or try it with smoked ham or mature Cheddar and crackers.

miso and Parmesan

1 sheet of frozen ready-rolled puff pastry
2 tablespoons white miso paste
50 g unsalted butter, softened
30 g Parmesan cheese, finely grated
1 tablespoon toasted sesame seeds

a baking tray lined with baking paper

Makes about 24

Lay the pastry on a clean work surface and allow it to defrost just enough so that it can be unrolled without cracking.

Combine the miso and butter in a small bowl and spread about two-thirds of this mixture evenly over the pastry. Sprinkle two-thirds of the Parmesan over the top. Fold the pastry in half. Spread the remaining butter mixture on the pastry and sprinkle over the remaining cheese. Fold the pastry over again to make a long rectangle shape and gently press down on the pastry. Put the pastry on the prepared baking tray and then into the freezer for 30 minutes so that it can be cut easily.

When you are ready to cook the palmiers, preheat the oven to 200°C (400°F) Gas 6.

Using a sharp knife, cut the pastry into 1-cm wide slices. Put the slices, cut-side up, on the baking tray, sprinkle over the sesame seeds and bake in the preheated oven for about 15 minutes, until puffed and golden. Serve while still warm.

onion jam

3 tablespoons olive oil
2 large white onions, very thinly sliced
4 anchovy fillets in olive oil, drained (optional)
3 sprigs of fresh thyme
3 tablespoons soft brown sugar
65 ml red wine
1 sheet of frozen ready-rolled puff pastry

a baking tray lined with baking paper

Makes about 24

Put the oil in a heavy-based saucepan set over high heat. Add the onions, anchovies (if using) and thyme. When the onions start to sizzle, reduce the heat to low, cover and cook for 15 minutes, stirring often, until the onions start to caramelize and turn a golden colour. Stir in the sugar and red wine and cook over medium heat until the liquid has been absorbed and the onions are thick and a deep plum colour. Let cool.

Lay the pastry on a clean work surface and allow it to defrost just enough so that it can be unrolled without cracking.

Spread the onion jam mixture evenly over the pastry and loosely roll it up like a Swiss roll, but do not roll it too tightly. Put it on the prepared baking tray and then into the freezer for 30 minutes so that it can be cut easily.

When you are ready to cook the palmiers, preheat the oven to 200°C (400°F) Gas 6.

Using a sharp knife, cut the pastry into 1-cm wide slices. Put the slices, cut-side up, on the baking tray and bake in the preheated oven for about 15 minutes, until puffed and golden. Serve while still warm.

Kipfler crisps with sour cream and caviar dip

This recipe takes the humble potato to new heights. Gourmet crisps are made using firm, waxy potatoes which gives them a lovely golden colour and buttery flavour. They are good enough to enjoy on their own but a real treat served this way. You don't have to buy expensive caviar – salmon pearls (roe) are my favourite; it's the salty flavour burst followed by the creamy indulgence of sour cream that's delicious.

800 g Kipfler potatoes (about 8) or other small waxy potato
125 ml olive oil
125 ml vegetable oil
250 ml sour cream or crème fraîche
1 tablespoon snipped fresh chives
2–3 tablespoons caviar or salmon roe
sea salt flakes, to sprinkle

Serves 6–8

Cut the potatoes into slices about 2–3 mm thick. Bring a large saucepan of lightly salted water to the boil. Add the potatoes, cover the pan and remove from the heat. Leave in the hot water for 5 minutes. Drain well and arrange the potatoes on a wire rack in a single layer until completely cool.

Put the oils in a saucepan or large frying pan set over high heat. When the oil is hot, cook the potato slices in batches for 5–6 minutes each, turning once or twice, until crisp and golden. Remove from the oil using a metal slotted spoon and drain on kitchen paper.

Put the crisps in a bowl, sprinkle liberally with sea salt flakes and toss to coat. Combine the sour cream and chives in a small bowl, top with the caviar and serve with the crisps on the side for dipping.

salmon rillettes with Melba toast

A rillette is a very traditional way of potting and preserving meats, such as pork or duck in fat. Here is a lighter, healthier and fuss-free version of this French classic. Some recipes call for the salmon to be steamed or poached, then flaked and mixed in with the other ingredients, but I find that cooking it in a paper parcel traps all the healthy oils and retains more flavour. That means there is less need to add other ingredients and you still get a very tasty result.

300 g salmon fillet (smoked if liked), skinned and pin-boned
50 g unsalted butter, chilled and cut into cubes
½ teaspoon sea salt
1 lemon, 1 half sliced and the other juiced
1 tablespoon finely chopped fresh dill
2 tablespoons snipped fresh chives
4 slices of white bread

Serves 4

Preheat the oven to 220°C (425°F) Gas 7.

Put the salmon on a sheet of baking paper large enough to wrap the fish entirely. Distribute the butter cubes evenly over the fish, sprinkle with the sea salt, add the lemon slices and finish with the dill. Firmly wrap up the fish in the paper, put it on a baking tray and cook in the preheated oven for 10 minutes. Leave in the paper and let cool to room temperature.

Remove the fish from the paper and pour any collected oil and juices into a large bowl. Discard the lemon slices. Flake the fish and put it in the bowl with the juices then add the chives and the lemon juice. Cover and refrigerate until needed.

To make the Melba toasts, preheat the grill to high and trim the crusts off the bread. Toast the bread on both sides until golden. Using a serrated knife, carefully cut each slice widthways to make 8 very thin slices. Cut each slice into 4 small triangles, return these to the grill and toast the uncooked side until golden. Serve alongside the salmon rillettes.

See photograph on page 32.

smoked trout, celeriac and apple salad

Here is a simple combination of ingredients that meld together to make a deliciously fresh-tasting salad. It's a salad in the coleslaw sense of the word and is best eaten spooned onto crisp little toasts.

200 g celeriac, peeled and grated
185 ml good-quality mayonnaise
1 tablespoon freshly squeezed lemon juice
1 smoked trout fillet, about 300 g
2 sweet eating apples, such as Red Delicious, cut into wedges
2 teaspoons finely chopped fresh tarragon
2 tablespoons finely chopped fresh flat leaf parsley
½ teaspoon smoked paprika (pimentón)
1 baguette, to serve

Serves 4–6

Combine the celeriac, mayonnaise and lemon juice in a bowl.

Peel the skin from the trout and discard. Roughly flake the fish into a separate mixing bowl. Add the apple wedges, tarragon, parsley, paprika and the celeriac mixture. Gently toss to combine without breaking up the fish too much. Spoon into a serving bowl.

Preheat the grill. Finely slice the baguette. Toast on both sides until golden. Cut into triangles and serve alongside the salad.

See photograph on page 33.

spiced red wine

2 tablespoons caster sugar
2 cardamom pods, lightly crushed
7 cinnamon sticks
1 bottle (750 ml) red wine

Serves 6

Combine the sugar, 125 ml water, cardamom pods and one of the cinnamon sticks in a small saucepan. Cook over low heat for 5 minutes, stirring to dissolve the sugar. Let cool, then refrigerate until chilled. Remove the spices.

Put the remaining 6 cinnamon sticks in 6 serving glasses and add the spiced syrup. Top up with the red wine.

pork and chicken liver terrine with pistachios

While I am all for abandoning the traditional notions of entertaining, some classics do still fit the bill. A terrine is perfect for sharing. It can also be made well in advance and, once served up, there is no fuss. Simply provide everyone with a knife and lay out some good bread and dishes of pickles.

1 kg pork mince
200 g dry-cured pork lardons
300 g chicken livers, roughly chopped
1 garlic clove, crushed
finely grated zest of 1 orange
2 teaspoons fennel seeds
50 g pistachios
1 egg, beaten
a handful of fresh flat leaf parsley leaves, finely chopped
12 bacon rashers
cornichons (baby gherkins) and any sweet pickle, to serve
1 baguette, to serve

a loaf tin or terrine dish, 20 x 10 x 7 cm, lightly oiled
a large, shallow baking dish or roasting tin

Serves 10–12

Put the pork mince, lardons, chicken livers, garlic, orange zest, fennel seeds and pistachios in a mixing bowl. Use your hands to combine thoroughly. Cover and refrigerate for at least 6 hours, preferably overnight, mixing occasionally.

Preheat the oven to 180°C (350°F) Gas 4.

Add the egg to the pork mixture and use your hands to thoroughly combine. Use the bacon rashers to line the loaf tin, ensuring that the ends of the rashers overhang the sides of the tin.

Spoon the pork mixture into the tin, pressing it down into the tin. The filling may be higher than the top of the tin at this stage, but it will settle during cooking. Cover the top of the loaf tin firmly with 2 layers of foil. Put the tin in the large, shallow baking dish. Add enough hot water to come halfway up the sides of the loaf tin. Cook in the preheated oven for 3 hours.

Remove the terrine from the baking dish and let it cool completely, leaving the foil intact. When cool, remove the foil and carefully turn the terrine out onto a serving plate or board. Cover and refrigerate until ready to enjoy. Serve with the pickles and sliced baguette.

cheap and cheerful

rosemary risotto with roasted summer vegetables

Most of us will be familiar with making a risotto, so there are no surprises here. When entertaining I don't like to be away from the table for too long, but it's possible to make the process of cooking a risotto a shared thing, especially now that so many home kitchens are part of the dining or living area. I've used fresh, seasonal ingredients here; summer vine vegetables are in abundance at the markets through until most of the autumn. If you want to cook an equally cheap and cheerful version of this risotto in the colder months, try roasting pumpkin, butternut squash or baby carrots until tender and serve them alongside the risotto.

3 tablespoons olive oil

1 tablespoon balsamic vinegar

12 small vine tomatoes

8 baby courgettes, halved lengthways

a bunch of thin asparagus spears, trimmed and halved

12 button mushrooms, stalks removed

1.25 litres vegetable or chicken stock

125 ml dry white wine

2 tablespoons butter

1 onion, chopped

1 garlic clove, chopped

1 teaspoon finely chopped fresh rosemary

330 g arborio (risotto) rice

100 g Parmesan cheese, finely grated

sea salt and freshly ground black pepper

Serves 4

Preheat the oven to 180°C (350°F) Gas 4.

Put 2 tablespoons of the olive oil and the balsamic vinegar in a large mixing bowl and whisk with a fork to combine. Add the tomatoes, courgettes, asparagus and mushrooms and toss to coat. Arrange the vegetables on a baking tray, pour over any liquid from the bowl and cook in the preheated oven for 40 minutes, turning after about 20 minutes. Set aside while cooking the risotto.

Put the stock and wine in a saucepan set over low heat.

Put the remaining oil and 1 tablespoon of the butter in a large, heavy-based frying pan set over medium heat and cook the onion, garlic and rosemary for 2–3 minutes, until softened. Add the rice and stir for 1 minute until the rice is glossy.

Add about 125 ml of the hot stock to the rice and cook, stirring constantly, until the rice has absorbed almost all the stock. Repeat until all the stock has been used and the rice is tender yet still retains a firmness to the bite. Stir through half of the Parmesan and the remaining butter and season to taste with salt and pepper. Cover, remove from the heat and let sit for 5 minutes before serving.

Serve the risotto with the roasted vegetables arranged on the side and the remaining Parmesan sprinkled over the top.

home-made potato gnocchi with roasted tomato sauce

Surprisingly, humble tinned tomatoes, when roasted, produce a thick, richly coloured sauce. This recipe has become a firm favourite and I use it as a base for many dishes. It's a good option when seasonal fresh tomatoes are not at their prime. Do try and use the best-quality tinned tomatoes you can find.

2 large floury potatoes, about 400 g each, unscrubbed

1 egg yolk

2 tablespoons very finely grated Parmesan cheese

125–150 g plain flour

1 teaspoon sea salt

Parmesan cheese shavings, to serve

a handful of fresh basil leaves, to garnish

roasted tomato sauce:

2 x 400-g tins whole plum tomatoes

2 red onions, chopped

4 garlic cloves, chopped

1 tablespoon soft brown sugar

3 tablespoons olive oil

extra virgin olive oil, to drizzle

sea salt

Serves 4

Preheat the oven to 180°C (350°F) Gas 4.

To make the sauce, put the tomatoes and any juice from the tins in a roasting tin with the onions, garlic, sugar and olive oil and sprinkle with a little sea salt. Cook in the preheated oven for 40–45 minutes, stirring after 20 minutes, until thick and deep red in colour. Transfer to a food processor and process until just combined to make a thick, chunky sauce. Set aside until needed.

To make the gnocchi, preheat the oven to 180°C (350°F) Gas 4. Prick the potatoes all over with a fork and put them directly on the middle shelf of the oven. Bake for 1–1½ hours, until the skin is browned and puffed. Remove, cover with a clean tea towel and set aside until cool enough to handle but still warm. The potato flesh needs to be warm for a light gnocchi.

Peel and discard the skin from the potatoes, then roughly chop the flesh. Put the chopped potato in a large bowl and mash until smooth (do not use a food processor or the gnocchi will be tough). Mix in the egg yolk, Parmesan and salt. Gradually stir in the flour – you may not need all of it, so add a little at a time until the dough is soft, pliable and damp but not sticky.

Using lightly floured hands, divide the gnocchi dough into 4 portions of equal size. Lightly flour the work surface. Use your hands to roll each portion into a log about 1½ cm in diameter. Using a sharp knife, cut each log into 1½-cm thick discs, then gently press the back of a fork into each gnocchi to make an indentation.

Bring a large saucepan of lightly salted water to the boil for the gnocchi. Meanwhile, gently reheat the sauce in a small saucepan set over low heat.

Cook the gnocchi in the boiling water for about 2 minutes, until they have risen to the surface and are tender. Drain well, transfer to serving plates and spoon over the warmed sauce. Serve sprinkled with Parmesan and scatter a few basil leaves over the top.

mushroom, spinach and potato bake

This is by no means a token vegetarian option – it is hearty, comforting and tasty, and will satisfy the hungriest of guests. And like many of the recipes in this chapter, it can be baked and served in the same dish. Fontina is a dense, nutty Italian cheese that melts beautifully and gives the mashed potatoes a delicious golden crust.

1 kg floury potatoes

125 ml full-fat milk

a pinch of freshly grated nutmeg

125 g butter, cut into cubes

500 g small chestnut mushrooms, left whole and stalks removed

4 garlic cloves, roughly chopped

4 spring onions, cut into 2-cm lengths

1 kg fresh spinach, well washed and roughly chopped

200 g fontina cheese, cubed

sea salt and freshly ground black pepper

a large, shallow baking dish

Serves 4–6

Peel and roughly chop the potatoes. Put them in a large saucepan of lightly salted boiling water and boil for about 12–15 minutes, until tender but not falling apart. Drain well, return to the warm pan and roughly mash. Add the milk and nutmeg and season to taste with salt and pepper. Beat with a large wooden spoon or hand-held electric whisk until smooth. Stir through half of the butter, until well combined. Spoon about one-third of the mixture into the baking dish.

Preheat the oven to 180°C (350°F) Gas 4.

Heat half of the remaining butter in a large frying pan set over medium heat. Add the mushrooms, garlic and spring onions and gently fry for about 10 minutes, until golden. Spoon over the potato mixture in the baking dish.

Heat the remaining butter in the frying pan and cook the spinach for 5 minutes, stirring often, until just wilted and tender. Season to taste and spoon over the mushrooms in the baking dish.

Spoon the remaining mashed potatoes on top of the spinach and scatter over the fontina. Bake in the preheated oven for about 30 minutes, until the cheese is bubbly and golden.

Next time: Swiss chard could be used instead of the spinach, making sure the tough stalks have been removed. Also, try adding 200 g sliced, chargrilled artichoke hearts, available from most delis and supermarkets, and add these after the mushrooms have been cooked off.

naked spinach and ricotta ravioli with sage cream

I call these little balls of spinach and ricotta 'naked' ravioli, as they are missing the pasta wrapping that usually encloses the filling. They look rather smart and could easily have appeared in the Chic chapter of this book, but they are in fact a good option for anyone on a budget, as they require just a few simple ingredients. They can be made a day in advance and chilled in the fridge until you are ready to cook them.

1 kg fresh spinach, well washed and roughly chopped

250 g ricotta

5 egg yolks

125 g Parmesan cheese, finely grated, plus extra to serve

125 g plain flour

1 tablespoon butter

12 fresh sage leaves

250 ml single cream

sea salt and freshly ground black pepper

a baking tray lined with baking paper

Serves 3–4

Bring a large saucepan of water to the boil. Add the spinach and cook for 5 minutes, until wilted and tender. Rinse with cold water and drain well.

Tip the cooked spinach into the centre of a clean tea towel. (This process will stain the tea towel so use an old, threadbare one, rather than your best.) Roll the tea towel up to form a log and twist the ends away from each other to squeeze out as much liquid as possible. Put the spinach on a chopping board and chop finely. Transfer to a large bowl. Add the ricotta, egg yolks and half of the Parmesan and season to taste with salt and pepper. Mix well to thoroughly combine.

Put the flour on a large plate. Using slightly wet hands, roll the spinach mixture into 12 walnut-sized balls. Lightly roll each ball in the flour and put them on the prepared baking tray.

Put the butter and sage in a small saucepan and set over medium heat. Cook until the sage leaves just sizzle. Add the cream and the remaining Parmesan and cook for about 10 minutes, until thickened, stirring often to prevent the cream from catching on the bottom of the pan.

Bring a large saucepan of lightly salted water to the boil. Carefully drop the balls into the boiling water and cook for just 1 minute, until they rise to the surface. Drain well and arrange 4 balls in each serving dish. Spoon over the warm sage cream, sprinkle with the extra Parmesan and grind over plenty of black pepper. Serve immediately.

fresh mussels with fennel aioli

Although you can buy ready-cooked and flavoured, vacuum-packed mussels, it's so much better from both a cost and a flavour point of view to buy them really fresh and clean them yourself. Most of their sold weight is shell, but when cooked in a tasty broth and served with bread on the side they are surprisingly filling, and made for sharing. Eating them always creates a lot of mess, but that's all part of the fun!

1 kg fresh mussels

2 small fennel bulbs, with feathery tops intact and reserved for aioli

1 tablespoon olive oil

1 tablespoon butter

1 garlic clove, finely chopped

1 small onion or 2 shallots, finely chopped

125 ml dry white wine

250 ml fish stock

2 ripe tomatoes, diced

a handful of fresh flat leaf parsley, roughly chopped

2 baguettes, to serve

fennel aioli:

reserved fennel tops (see above)

185 ml good-quality mayonnaise

3 garlic cloves, crushed

Serves 4

Scrub the mussels well, knock off any barnacles and pull off the beards. Discard any broken mussels and any that won't close when they are tapped on the work surface. Drain in a colander and set aside until needed.

To make the aioli, finely chop the feathery tops of the fennel and combine in a small bowl with the mayonnaise and garlic. Cover and chill until needed.

Finely chop the fennel bulbs. Heat the olive oil and butter in a large stockpot or saucepan set over medium heat and gently cook the garlic, onion and fennel for about 10 minutes, until the fennel has softened.

Add the white wine, stock and tomatoes and bring to the boil. Cook for 5 minutes. Add the mussels, cover tightly with a lid and cook for a further 5 minutes, shaking the pan occasionally, until the mussels have opened. Discard any that don't open. Add the parsley and stir.

Spoon the mussels into deep serving bowls and put an empty bowl on the table for discarded shells. Offer the fennel aioli on the side for spooning and a basket of warmed, sliced baguette.

Next time: For a tasty alternative, try adding 1 finely diced chorizo sausage to the pan when cooking off the garlic, onion and fennel.

Moroccan-style white fish and heirloom tomato tagine

I like to use blue-eye in this recipe – it's a fish that's local to me here in Australia and I can often buy it at a good price. It may not be as readily available or inexpensive where you are, so cod, monkfish or any other firm, white fish fillet will do just fine. This dish typifies the simplicity of traditional Moroccan cooking techniques and is full of aromatic spices. Using flavourful, ripe tomatoes will make all the difference, so this is best enjoyed in the summer. Serve with buttery couscous or a crisp, green salad.

5 garlic cloves

1 teaspoon sea salt

2 teaspoons ground cumin

1 teaspoon paprika

1 tablespoon freshly squeezed lemon juice

a small bunch of fresh coriander, finely chopped

3 tablespoons olive oil

750 g any firm white fish fillet, such as cod or monkfish

3 large ripe tomatoes, roughly chopped

8 small waxy potatoes, sliced

a handful of small black olives, stoned

a handful of fresh coriander leaves, to garnish

couscous, to serve

Serves 4

Crush 2 of the garlic cloves and combine them in a large, non-reactive bowl with the salt, cumin, paprika, lemon juice, coriander and 1 tablespoon of the oil.

Cut the fish into large chunks and put them in the bowl with the garlic mixture. Gently toss the fish until it is evenly coated. Cover and let sit at cool room temperature for 1 hour.

Heat the remaining oil in a frying pan set over medium heat and cook the remaining garlic, finely chopped, for 1 minute. Add the tomatoes and stir-fry for about 2–3 minutes until softened.

Add the potato slices and 250 ml water. Bring to the boil and cook for 5 minutes. Add the fish pieces to the pan, reduce the heat to a low simmer, cover tightly with a lid and cook for about 15 minutes, until the fish is cooked through and the potatoes are tender. Stir in the olives and season to taste. Spoon over couscous and garnish with a few coriander leaves to serve.

Thai-style fish with smoky tomato relish

This is an authentic Thai treat you can easily replicate at home. The tasty tomato relish is also great served with grilled chicken or gently heated and stirred through some cooked prawns.

3 ripe tomatoes

2 large red chillies

1 whole garlic bulb, unpeeled

6 shallots, unpeeled

1 tablespoon freshly squeezed lemon juice

2 tablespoons Thai fish sauce

4 long stalks of fresh coriander, with roots intact

4 garlic cloves, chopped

½ teaspoon black peppercorns

4 x 200-g white fish fillets, such as cod, hake, haddock or sea bass

lime halves or wedges, for squeezing

a baking tray lined with baking paper

Serves 4

Preheat the oven to 220°C (425°F) Gas 7.

Put the tomatoes, chillies, garlic bulb and shallots in a roasting tin and cook in the preheated oven for 10–15 minutes. Remove the tin from the oven, transfer the chillies, garlic and shallots to a bowl and cover. (This will make them sweat and therefore be easier to peel.) Return the tomatoes to the oven for a further 5 minutes, then add them to the bowl with the other vegetables and cover.

When cool enough to handle, peel the tomatoes and chillies and put the flesh in a food processor. Squeeze the soft flesh of the shallots and garlic out of their skins and add. Blend to make a chunky sauce. Stir in the lemon juice and 1 tablespoon of the fish sauce and set aside.

Reduce the oven temperature to 180°C (350°F) Gas 4. Cut off the coriander roots, clean and roughly chop. Reserve a few leaves to garnish and chop the remaining leaves and stalks. Put the roots in a mortar with the garlic cloves, peppercorns and remaining fish sauce and pound with a pestle to make a paste. Put the fish fillets on the prepared baking tray. Spread a quarter of the coriander paste over each fillet. Cook in the preheated oven for 20 minutes. Serve with the relish spooned over the top and lime halves on the side for squeezing. Garnish with the reserved coriander leaves.

chicken pot pies

The filling for these comforting pies is made with ready-cooked rotisserie chicken (now available at most large supermarkets). I don't know where I would be without it! The flesh can be shredded and used warm or cold in salads or diced and added to soups, stir-fries and pasta sauces. Don't discard the bones – these can be kept and used to make stock.

1 small rotisserie chicken

3 tablespoons butter

1 leek, sliced

1 carrot, diced

1 celery stick, diced

125 ml dry white wine

3 tablespoons plain flour

500 ml chicken stock

100 g frozen peas

125 ml single cream

1 sheet ready-rolled puff pastry, defrosted if frozen

1 egg yolk, beaten with 1 tablespoon water

sea salt and freshly ground black pepper

4 baking dishes, each about 250 ml capacity

Serves 4

Preheat the oven to 180°C (350°F) Gas 4.

Remove the skin from the chicken, slice the meat off the bones and chop finely. Set aside until needed.

Melt the butter in a large saucepan set over high heat and add the leek, carrot and celery. Sauté for 5 minutes, until softened. Add the wine and cook for a further 5 minutes, until it has almost evaporated. Add the chicken and stir well to combine. Sprinkle the flour into the pan. Cook for 1 minute, then gradually pour in the stock, stirring constantly as you do so. Bring to the boil and cook uncovered, stirring often, for 2–3 minutes, until the mixture has thickened. Add the peas and cream to the pan and stir well. Cook for 1 minute, then remove from the heat. Season to taste with salt and pepper and let cool to room temperature.

Spoon the mixture into the baking dishes. Unroll the pastry and lay it on a lightly floured work surface. Use a sharp knife to cut circles from the pastry just slightly larger than the top of the dishes. Put a pastry circle on top of each dish, folding the pastry over the side and pressing down firmly with the tines of a fork. Brush with the egg wash and cook in the preheated oven for about 25–30 minutes, until the pastry is puffed and golden.

See photographs on pages 52–53.

Vietnamese chicken curry

The inclusion of both bay leaves and lemongrass here may seem a tad odd, but Vietnamese cuisine has been strongly influenced by French cooking styles. I once ate a curry in Vietnam that was served in a big bowl placed in the centre of the table, along with a crusty baguette – there wasn't a grain of rice to be seen!

1 chicken, about 1.8 kg, cut into 10–12 pieces

2 tablespoons mild curry powder

3 tablespoons light olive oil

2 onions, cut into thick wedges

3 garlic cloves, roughly chopped

1 lemongrass stalk, gently bruised

3 dried or fresh bay leaves

2 carrots, each cut into 4 thick chunks

2 x 400-ml tins coconut milk

½ teaspoon caster sugar

sea salt and freshly ground black pepper

1–2 baguettes, to serve

a flameproof casserole (optional)

Serves 4

Put the chicken pieces in a large bowl. Add the curry powder, 1 teaspoon sea salt and some black pepper. Use your hands to toss the chicken until it is evenly coated in the curry mixture.

Put 1 tablespoon of the oil in a casserole or large, heavy-based saucepan and set over medium heat. Add half of the chicken pieces and cook for 5 minutes, turning often, until golden brown and crisp. Transfer to a plate. Add another tablespoon of oil to the pan and cook the remaining chicken pieces in the same way. Add them to the first batch. Add the remaining tablespoon of oil to the pan and add the onions, garlic and lemongrass. Cook for 5 minutes, until the onions are golden and soft, stirring occasionally.

Add the bay leaves and carrots to the pan and cook for 2–3 minutes. Increase the heat to high. Add the coconut milk and sugar and bring to the boil, stirring often. Reduce the heat to medium. Cook for 10 minutes. Add all the chicken pieces, except any from the breast, and cook for 10 minutes. The liquid should be gently simmering, not rapidly boiling. Add the remaining chicken and any collected juices and cook for a further 10 minutes, until the chicken is cooked through. Serve with fresh baguette.

chicken shish kebabs with garlic sauce

Like most Middle-Eastern foods these kebabs are perfect for sharing. The garlic sauce is simple to make using easy-to-source ingredients and will keep refrigerated in an airtight container for several days.

125 ml extra virgin olive oil

4 garlic cloves, crushed

65 ml freshly squeezed lemon juice

2½ tablespoons finely chopped flat leaf parsley

1 kg chicken thigh fillets, trimmed and cubed

4 handfuls of any soft green salad leaves

2 tomatoes, cut into wedges

1 cucumber, peeled and sliced

8 soft wheat flour tortillas, to serve

lemons wedges, to serve

sea salt and freshly ground black pepper

garlic sauce:

12 garlic cloves, coarsely chopped

125 ml olive oil

1 teaspoon sea salt

125 ml good-quality mayonnaise

1 tablespoon freshly squeezed lemon juice

10–12 wooden skewers, soaked in cold water

Serves 4

To make the garlic sauce, put the garlic and salt in a small food processor and process until finely chopped. Add the mayonnaise. With the motor still running, add the olive oil in a very slow trickle, until all of the oil has been incorporated and the sauce is smooth. Stir in the lemon juice and season to taste with black pepper.

Put the olive oil, garlic, lemon juice, parsley and 1 teaspoon salt in a large, non-reactive bowl and whisk with a fork. Add the chicken and use your hands to toss until evenly coated. Season well and cover with clingfilm. Let sit at cool room temperature for 1 hour.

Preheat the grill to medium/high. Thread the chicken onto the prepared skewers. Cook the kebabs for 4–5 minutes, turning occasionally, until the chicken is golden and cooked through.

Arrange the salad leaves, tomatoes and cucumber on serving plates. Put the kebabs on top and drizzle with the sauce. Serve with warmed tortillas and lemon wedges for squeezing.

See photographs on pages 56–57.

coq au left-over red wine

Although any left-over red wine will do for this recipe, I love using pinot noir. It may not be that cheap but if you have genuine leftovers that are no longer drinkable, it's better to put them to good use than to waste them. I am a big fan of the chicken drumstick in recipes that typically call for a whole bird to be cut into portions. It saves you some chopping and you can more easily calculate portion size and keep the cost down – I would usually allow two drumsticks per person. Bear in mind that the chicken marinates in the wine overnight, so you'll need to start prepping the day before you intend to serve. The perfect accompaniment is garlic mash.

8 chicken drumsticks

250 ml pinot noir or any other red wine

1 onion, chopped

1 carrot, diced

1 celery stick, diced

4 garlic cloves, sliced

1 dried or fresh bay leaf

4 tablespoons olive oil

12 pickling onions or small shallots

4 bacon rashers, roughly chopped

100 g button mushrooms, stalks removed

500 ml beef stock

sea salt and freshly ground black pepper

garlic mash:
800 g floury potatoes, peeled and quartered or halved, depending on size

125 ml full-fat milk

3 garlic cloves, crushed

75 g butter

a large, flameproof casserole (optional)

Serves 4

Put the chicken drumsticks in a non-reactive dish with the red wine, onion, carrot, celery, garlic and bay leaf. Cover and refrigerate overnight, turning occasionally. Set a colander over a large bowl and tip the entire contents of the dish into it. Remove the chicken drumsticks and leave the vegetables in the colander to drain. Reserve the marinating liquid.

Heat 1 tablespoon of the oil in a casserole or large, heavy-based saucepan and cook the pickling onions and bacon for 4–5 minutes, shaking the pan often, until golden. Remove from the pan and set aside. Add another tablespoon of the oil to the pan and cook the mushrooms for 5 minutes, until golden and softened. Remove from the pan and set aside.

Add another tablespoon of the oil to the pan and cook half of the chicken drumsticks for a few minutes until well browned all over. Transfer to a plate. Add the remaining oil and drumsticks to the pan and repeat. Add the drained vegetables, garlic and bay leaf to the pan and cook for 5 minutes, until softened and golden.

Return the chicken, pickling onions and bacon to the pan along with the reserved marinating liquid and the beef stock. Bring to the boil, then reduce the heat to medium, cover and cook for about 20 minutes, until the chicken is cooked through and tender. Add the mushrooms and cook for another 5 minutes.

Meanwhile, to make the garlic mash, cook the potatoes in a large saucepan of lightly salted boiling water for 15 minutes, until very tender. Drain well and return to the warm pan. Put the milk, garlic and butter in a small saucepan and cook over low heat until melted. Add the milk mixture to the potatoes and mash or beat until smooth and fluffy. Season to taste. Serve with the chicken casserole.

spicy pork curry with lemon rice

It's useful to have a curry recipe to hand that does not require a vast number of different spices. With the exception of the ground cumin, the curry paste that forms the basis of this recipe calls for fresh ingredients. If pork is not your thing, simply replace it with the same quantity of a stewing steak like chuck – the cooking time will be the same.

2 tomatoes, chopped

2 large green chillies, chopped

4 garlic cloves

1 onion, chopped

2 teaspoons ground cumin

5-cm piece of fresh ginger, grated

a small bunch of fresh coriander, roots and stalks roughly chopped and leaves reserved to garnish

2 tablespoons vegetable oil

750 g pork shoulder, cut into bite-sized pieces

2 tablespoons white vinegar

very finely shredded fresh ginger, to garnish

lemon rice:

400 g basmati rice

½ teaspoon turmeric

3 tablespoons butter

4–6 dried curry leaves

½ teaspoon brown mustard seeds

2 teaspoons finely grated lemon zest

1 tablespoon freshly squeezed lemon juice

a flameproof casserole (optional)

Serves 4

Put the tomatoes, chillies, garlic, onion, cumin, ginger, coriander roots and stalks and oil in a food processor and process until smooth. Put the paste in a flameproof casserole or heavy-based saucepan and set over medium heat. Cook for 5 minutes, stirring constantly, until golden and aromatic.

Put the pork in the casserole, add 1 litre water and bring to the boil, stirring occasionally. Reduce the heat to low so that the liquid just gently simmers and cook, uncovered, for 1½ hours, stirring often so that the meat doesn't catch and burn. Stir in the vinegar.

Meanwhile, to make the lemon rice, rinse the rice in several changes of cold water. Bring a large saucepan of water to the boil and add the turmeric. Add the rice and cook for 10–12 minutes, until tender. Drain well and return to the warm pan. Heat the butter in a small saucepan set over high heat and cook the curry leaves and mustard seeds until they start to sizzle. Add to the rice along with the lemon zest and juice and stir well to combine.

To serve, garnish the curry with shredded ginger and the coriander leaves and serve with the lemon rice.

slow-cooked spiced pork belly with apple and fennel

I prefer to use pork belly here, but you could also roast a shoulder or leg joint of pork for this recipe. You can't go far wrong with this low-temperature, slow-cooking method, which produces crispy skin and melt-in-the-mouth meat. This is one of my favourite Saturday night specials – it greets your guests with a delicious aroma, creating a mood of anticipation, which is the key to good entertaining.

1 tablespoon fennel seeds

2 teaspoons caraway seeds

4 garlic cloves

2 tablespoons olive oil

1 kg pork belly

4 apples, such as Cox's Orange Pippin

2 fennel bulbs, with feathery tops intact, cut into thick wedges

sea salt and freshly ground black pepper

Serves 4

Combine the fennel and caraway seeds, garlic and 1 tablespoon salt in a mortar and pound with a pestle. Stir in 1 tablespoon of the olive oil.

Cut ½-cm deep incisions, spaced 1–2 cm apart, across the skin of the pork. Rub the spice mixture into the incisions, and let sit for 1 hour at cool room temperature.

Preheat the oven to 140°C (275°F) Gas 1.

Put the pork in a large roasting tin and cook in the preheated oven for 3 hours in total. (You'll need to remove the tin from the oven 30 minutes before the end of the cooking time to add the apples and fennel.)

Put the remaining oil in a large bowl and season with a little salt and pepper. Add the apples and the fennel bulbs with feathery tops to the bowl and use your hands to toss until evenly coated in oil. Thirty minutes before the end of the cooking time, remove the pork from the oven and arrange the apples and fennel in the tin. Increase the heat to 220°C (425°F) Gas 7 and return the tin to the oven.

Remove the pork from the oven, cover loosely with foil and let rest for about 20 minutes. Carve into slices and serve with the roasted apples and fennel on the side.

beef daube

This is definitely not fast food, so relax and let the ingredients and your oven do all the work. You can use a cheaper cut of meat here and it will still taste good after a long marinating and cooking time.

750 g chuck steak, in one large piece
1 large carrot, diced
1 celery stick, diced
1 fresh or dried bay leaf
3 garlic cloves, unpeeled and smashed
500 ml red wine
1 tablespoon olive oil
1 tablespoon butter, plus extra for peas
400-g tin chopped tomatoes
250 ml beef stock
400 g dried pasta tubes, such as rigatoni
130 g frozen baby peas
50 g Parmesan cheese, finely grated
sea salt and freshly ground black pepper

a large, flameproof casserole

Serves 6–8

Put the beef in a non-reactive dish with the carrot, celery, bay leaf, garlic and red wine. Cover and refrigerate overnight, turning occasionally. Set a colander over a large bowl and tip the entire contents of the dish into it. Remove the meat and leave the vegetables in the colander to drain. Reserve the marinating liquid.

Heat the oil and butter in a casserole set over medium/high heat. Add the beef and cook for 8 minutes, turning every 2 minutes, until very dark. Remove from the pan. Add the carrot, celery, bay leaf and garlic to the pan and cook for 5 minutes, until the carrot is tender. Add the reserved marinating liquid and cook for about 8–10 minutes, until the liquid has reduced by half and become aromatic.

Return the beef to the pan with the tomatoes and stock. Bring to the boil, then reduce the heat to a gentle simmer. Partially cover and cook for 1 hour, until the meat is tender. Remove the meat from the pan and roughly shred it with a fork. Boil the sauce for 10 minutes, until thickened. Return the meat to the pan and season to taste with salt and pepper. Keep warm until ready to serve.

Cook the pasta according to the packet instructions. Drain and return it to the warm saucepan. Cook the peas until tender. Drain and return to the warm saucepan with 1 tablespoon butter, stirring until it has melted. Combine the beef and pasta and serve with the peas spooned over the top and a sprinkle of grated Parmesan.

beef pie

Beef pie is the national dish of Australia, so I had to include one! All you need with this is mash and peas.

500 g chuck steak, cut into bite-sized pieces
3 tablespoons plain flour
50 g butter
2 onions, chopped
2 tablespoons olive oil
250 ml beer
500 ml beef stock
2 tablespoons Worcestershire sauce
1 tablespoon light soy sauce
350-g pack ready-made shortcrust pastry, defrosted if frozen
1 egg yolk, beaten with 1 tablespoon water

a ceramic pie dish

Serves 4

Put the beef in a colander. Sprinkle with the flour and use your hands to toss the pieces until they are coated in flour.

Heat the butter in a large, heavy-based saucepan set over medium/high heat. Add the onions and cook for 5 minutes, until golden. Remove from the pan and set aside. Add 1 tablespoon of the oil to the pan. Add half the beef and cook for 4–5 minutes, until browned all over. Remove from the pan and set aside. Add the remaining oil to the pan and repeat with the remaining beef.

Add the beer, stock and sauces to the pan and bring to the boil. Return the beef to the pan, cook briefly, then reduce the heat to low. Cover and cook for 1 hour, stirring occasionally. Add the onions and increase the heat to high. Boil for about 15–20 minutes, until the gravy is thick and dark. Let cool completely.

Preheat the oven to 200°C (400°F) Gas 6 and put a baking tray on the centre shelf of the oven.

Lightly flour a work surface. Roll the pastry out to a thickness of about 5 mm. Use a sharp knife to cut a circle slightly larger than the top of the pie dish. Re-roll the remaining pastry and use a knife to cut long strips about 1½ cm wide. Brush some of the egg wash around the rim of the pie dish and press the pastry strips around the edge. Brush the pastry with egg wash and put the pastry lid on top. Use a fork to press down around the edge to seal and brush all over the remaining egg wash. Bake in the preheated oven for about 45–50 minutes, until the pastry is golden and crisp.

See photograph on pages 66–67.

lamb kefta tagine with crunchy salad

If you are interested in cooking with spices, Moroccan food is a great place to start. This style of cooking uses a relatively short list of staple spices, such as cumin, cinnamon and cayenne pepper, but they are all used in varying quantities to produce very different results from one recipe to the next. A tagine is a Moroccan stew that's traditionally cooked in a large-lidded terracotta pot, which gives the dish its name. My version is made in a large frying pan and is an ideal, fuss-free one-pot dish.

500 g lamb mince

1 onion, grated

2 garlic cloves, finely chopped

a handful of fresh flat leaf parsley leaves, finely chopped

2 tablespoons olive oil

1 teaspoon ground cumin

1 teaspoon ground cinnamon

½ teaspoon cayenne pepper

400-g tin chopped tomatoes

a large handful of chopped fresh coriander leaves

crunchy salad:

1 small head of iceberg lettuce, shredded into 2-cm wide strips

1 small red onion, very thinly sliced

2 handfuls of fresh mint leaves

2 tablespoons olive oil

1 tablespoon freshly squeezed lemon juice

sea salt and freshly ground black pepper

Serves 4

Put the mince, half of the onion, half of the garlic and the parsley in a bowl. Use your hands to combine and throw the mixture against the side of the bowl several times. Set aside.

Heat the oil in a large heavy-based frying pan set over high heat and cook the remaining onion and garlic for 5 minutes, until softened and golden. Add the spices and cook, stirring constantly, for 1 minute, until aromatic. Add the tomatoes and 250 ml water and bring to the boil. Cook for about 5 minutes.

With slightly wet hands, roll the lamb mixture into walnut-sized balls and put them directly into the sauce mixture as you do so. Reduce the heat, cover and cook for about 15 minutes, until the mince is cooked through. Stir in the coriander and keep warm.

To make the salad, put the lettuce, onion and mint in a salad bowl and use your hands to toss. Pour over the olive oil and lemon juice and season to taste with salt and pepper. Serve the tagine with the crunchy salad on the side.

shepherd's pie

Old-school, traditional fare like shepherd's pie never goes out of style. If you want to make this a little smarter, bake it in individual ovenproof dishes, but I like the casualness of sitting the dish in the centre of the table and letting everyone help themselves.

2 tablespoons olive oil

125 g butter

2 large onions, chopped

2 carrots, grated

2 celery sticks, chopped

750 g lamb mince

1 litre beef stock

2½ tablespoons cornflour

a large handful of flat leaf parsley leaves, finely chopped

1 kg floury potatoes, peeled and quartered or halved, depending on size

85 ml milk

sea salt and freshly ground black pepper

a large ovenproof baking di

Serves 6

Heat the oil and 1 tablespoon of the butter in large, heavy-based frying pan set over high heat. When the butter has melted and is sizzling, add the onions and cook for 5 minutes, until golden. Add the carrots and celery and cook for a further 5 minutes. Add the mince and cook for 10 minutes, until it has browned, stirring often to break up any large clumps.

Put the cornflour in a small bowl and stir in 65 ml of the stock. Add the remaining stock to the pan with the mince and cook for 10 minutes, letting the stock boil and reduce a little. Add the cornflour mixture to the pan and cook, stirring constantly, until the liquid thickens to a gravy. Stir in the parsley, season well with salt and pepper and set aside.

Preheat the oven to 180°C (350°F) Gas 4.

Put the potatoes in a large saucepan of lightly salted boiling water. Cook for 10 minutes, until they are just starting to break up and the water is cloudy. Drain well and return to the warm pan. Add the remaining butter and the milk and season to taste with salt and pepper. Roughly mash to leave the potatoes with a chunky texture.

Spoon the mince into the baking dish and spread the mashed potatoes over the top. Cook in the preheated oven for about 40–45 minutes, until the potato is crisp and golden brown.

Next time: You could also use beef or pork mince as an alternative to the lamb. Try adding some thinly sliced leeks or finely chopped fennel bulbs when you are cooking the onions.

food in a flash

pappardelle pasta with roast fennel, tomato and olives

This technique of roasting vegetables in the oven makes easy work of a pasta sauce. The veggies soften and sweeten while they cook and there is no constant stirring involved as there is with hob-top cooking. If you can't find wide pasta ribbons (pappardelle), simply buy fresh lasagne sheets and cut them into 1½-cm strips.

65 ml extra virgin olive oil
4 tomatoes, halved
2 red onions, cut into wedges
4 small courgettes, thickly sliced
2 small fennel bulbs, thickly sliced
2 garlic cloves, thickly sliced
1 teaspoon smoked paprika (pimentón)
50 g small black olives
400 g fresh pappardelle pasta
2 tablespoons butter
salt and freshly ground black pepper
grated manchego cheese, to serve

Serves 4

Preheat the oven to 220°C (425°F) Gas 7.

Put the olive oil in a roasting tin and put it in the oven for 5 minutes to heat up.

Add all of the vegetables and the garlic to the roasting tin and sprinkle over the paprika. Season to taste with salt and pepper. Roast in the preheated oven for about 20 minutes, giving the tin a shake after 15 minutes. Remove from the oven and stir in the olives. Cover and let sit while you cook the pasta.

Bring a large saucepan of lightly salted water to the boil. Add the pasta and cook according to the packet instructions, or just until the pasta rises to the top – it will cook much quicker than dried pasta. Drain well and return to the warm pan. Add the butter and toss well. Add the roasted vegetables and toss gently to combine. Sprinkle with grated manchego to serve.

lime pickle and vegetable biryani

Here is a speedy recipe does not use the traditional biryani technique of frying the rice with the spices, adding the other ingredients and cooking it all together. Instead, the vegetables are stir-fried with a spicy curry paste and the cooked rice is then added. Do use the best lime pickle you can find. Some can be bitter beyond belief, while others are sour yet piquant and it's the latter you want to find. Don't stress about using the rice vermicelli, but it does give an authentic touch to an otherwise cheat's version of this classic Indian recipe.

2 tablespoon bottled lime pickle
1 onion, roughly chopped
2 garlic cloves
2 teaspoons grated fresh ginger
2 tablespoons olive oil
2 carrots, cut into thin batons
2 courgettes, cut into thin batons
370 g basmati rice
50 g dried rice vermicelli, broken into shorter lengths (optional)
a large handful of fresh mint leaves, larger leaves roughly torn
50 g toasted cashews, roughly chopped

Serves 4

Put the pickle, onion, garlic and ginger in a food processor and process to make a paste.

Heat the oil in a large, heavy-based saucepan set over medium heat. Add the paste and cook, stirring, for 2–3 minutes, until aromatic. Add the carrots and stir-fry for 2–3 minutes, until lightly golden. Add the courgettes and stir-fry for 2 minutes, then turn off the heat.

Bring a large saucepan of water to the boil. Add the rice and cook for 8–10 minutes, until just tender. Add the rice vermicelli, if using, and cook for another 2–3 minutes, stirring well so that the vermicelli does not stick together and is soft and transparent. Drain well.

Set the saucepan with the vegetables over high heat. Add the rice mixture and stir well until it takes on the golden colour of the curry paste. Stir in the mint and scatter with toasted cashews to serve.

See photograph on page 76.

fresh tomato, pea and paneer curry

I always prefer to cook a curry from a recipe that does not involve dozens and dozens of dry spices. Southern Indian food tends to have a greater emphasis on fresh ingredients, with just one or two spices thrown in, so this style of cooking appeals to me. Paneer is a firm, white cheese from India – if you can't find it, halloumi will work just as well.

2 tablespoons vegetable oil
250 g paneer, cubed
1 tablespoon butter
2 onions, finely chopped
5-cm piece of fresh ginger, grated
2 green chillies, deseeded and finely chopped
3 ripe tomatoes, roughly chopped
2 teaspoons white wine vinegar
200 g frozen peas
½ teaspoon garam masala
a handful of fresh coriander leaves
sea salt and freshly ground black pepper

to serve:
cooked basmati rice
naan bread
mango chutney

Serves 4

Heat the oil in a frying pan set over medium heat. Add the paneer and cook for 4–5 minutes, turning often, until golden all over. Remove from the pan and set aside.

Add the butter to the pan. When it is melted and sizzling, add the onions and stir-fry until softened and lightly golden. Add the ginger and chillies to the pan and cook for 1 minute.

Add the tomatoes, vinegar and 65 ml water and bring to the boil. Cook for about 5 minutes, to thicken slightly. Add the peas and return the paneer to the pan. Reduce the heat and simmer for about 5 minutes, until the peas are tender.

Stir in the garam masala and season to taste with salt and pepper. Sprinkle with the coriander leaves and serve with basmati rice and an assortment of Indian accompaniments.

See photograph on page 77.

smoked trout fattoush

Fattoush is a fresh-tasting salad from the Lebanon. Despite its exotic name, the ingredients are basically summer garden produce – cucumber, tomato, parsley and mint – with the addition of crisp pieces of toasted bread. All these foods go very well with smoked trout, one of my favourite deli foods that's often overlooked, so I've given it a break and added it to my interpretation of this recipe.

2 pitta breads or Indian chappatis
125 ml olive oil
1 smoked trout, about 450–500g
1 small head of cos lettuce, shredded
1 large cucumber, cut into thin batons
4 Roma tomatoes, halved and sliced
1 small red onion, thinly sliced
a large handful of fresh flat leaf parsley leaves, roughly chopped
a handful of fresh mint leaves, roughly chopped
3 tablespoons freshly squeezed lemon juice
2 teaspoons ground sumac (optional)

Serves 4

Preheat the oven to 180°C (350°F) Gas 4.

Split the pitta breads in half and brush lightly with some of the olive oil. Put on a baking tray and cook in the preheated oven for about 10 minutes, turning after 5 minutes, until golden. While still warm, break the bread into smaller pieces and set aside on a wire rack to cool and crisp up.

Carefully pull the skin off the trout and discard. Gently fork the flesh from the bones and flake into smaller pieces.

Put the lettuce, cucumber, tomato, onion and herbs in a large salad bowl. Add the trout and pitta bread pieces and gently toss to combine without breaking up the trout too much.

Put the remaining olive oil in a small bowl. Add the lemon juice and whisk with a fork to combine. Pour the dressing over the salad and sprinkle with sumac, if using. Serve immediately.

gnocchetti pasta with smoky chorizo and seared prawns

This is a lovely summery pasta dish, perfect for enjoying al fresco – it makes the effort of setting up a table outside completely worthwhile. Its influences are part Italian and part Spanish, which can only mean one thing: it's a sexy little number, just perfect for effortless entertaining.

200 g large raw prawns, peeled and deveined

1 tablespoon red wine vinegar

2 tablespoons olive oil

1 red onion, chopped

1 green pepper, deseeded and thinly sliced

100 g chorizo sausage, finely chopped

½ teaspoon smoked paprika (pimentón)

400-g tin chopped tomatoes

300 g dried gnocchetti or any other pasta shape, such as fusilli or penne

a handful of fresh mint leaves, chopped

a handful of fresh flat leaf parsley leaves, roughly chopped

sea salt and freshly ground black pepper

lemon wedges, to serve

Serves 4

Put the prawns in a non-reactive bowl with the vinegar and 1 tablespoon of the olive oil. Season with a little salt and pepper and set aside.

Heat the remaining olive oil in a heavy-based saucepan set over high heat. Add the onion, green pepper and chorizo and cook for 4–5 minutes, until softened and aromatic. Add the paprika and cook for 1 minute, stirring to combine. Add the tomatoes and 125 ml water and bring to the boil. Cook for 5 minutes, until the sauce has thickened slightly. Set aside while you cook the pasta.

Bring a large saucepan of lightly salted water to the boil. Add the pasta and cook for 12–15 minutes, until tender yet a little firm to the bite. Drain well and return to the warm pan. Add the tomato sauce and keep warm over very low heat while cooking the prawns.

Heat a non-stick frying pan over high heat. Cook the prawns for 2 minutes each side until pink.

Stir the prawns through the pasta and season to taste. Spoon onto serving plates and scatter the mint and parsley over each one. Serve with lemon wedges on the side for squeezing.

wholemeal pasta with courgette and mint

I love the nutty taste of wholemeal pasta and it works brilliantly here with the bright flavours of mint, chilli and lemon in a simple-to-assemble pasta dish. As the sauce relies on flavour rather than texture, this recipe does not work as well with other pasta shapes so it's best to stick to spaghetti or linguine.

400 g dried wholemeal spaghetti
65 ml olive oil
6 courgettes, grated
2 red onions, finely chopped
2 garlic cloves, roughly chopped
1 tablespoon freshly squeezed lemon juice
½ teaspoon dried chilli flakes
a large handful of fresh mint leaves, roughly chopped
a large handful of fresh flat leaf parsley leaves, roughly chopped
freshly grated Parmesan cheese, to serve
sea salt

Serves 4

Bring a large saucepan of lightly salted water to the boil. Add the pasta and cook for 10–12 minutes, until tender.

Meanwhile, heat the olive oil in a large, heavy-based frying pan set over medium heat. Add the courgettes and onions and cook, stirring, for about 10 minutes, until softened and turning golden.

Add the garlic, lemon juice and chilli flakes and cook for 1 minute further. Remove from the heat.

Drain the pasta well and add to the pan with the courgette mixture. Add the herbs and toss well to combine. Serve immediately, sprinkled with Parmesan cheese.

pasta salad with tuna, chilli and rocket

I really don't know why tinned fish gets such a bad press – it is one of the most convenient and healthy fast foods to have on hand. I just love it with other simple, fresh Mediterranean flavours, such as lemon and parsley. The inclusion of feta cheese here may seem a little odd, but it really does work. Just a small amount provides an extra tangy, savoury element to this summery dish. Any large, open pasta shape will work, but I have used lumaconi here, which translated from the Italian means 'big snail shells'.

400 g large dried pasta shells, such as lumaconi
65 ml olive oil
2 red onions, finely chopped
2 garlic cloves, finely chopped
1 large red chilli, deseeded and finely chopped
2 tablespoons small salted capers, rinsed
1 tablespoon red wine vinegar
400-g tin tuna chunks in oil, well drained
50 g feta cheese, crumbled
50 g wild rocket
sea salt and freshly ground black pepper
lemon wedges, to serve

Serves 4

Bring a large saucepan of lightly salted water to the boil. Add the pasta and cook for 8–10 minutes, until tender. Drain well and add 1 tablespoon of the olive oil. Transfer to a large bowl.

Heat the remaining oil in a large frying pan set over high heat. Add the onions, garlic, chilli and capers and cook, stirring, for 2–3 minutes, until the onion has softened. Add the vinegar and cook for a further minute. Add the tuna and use a fork to roughly break up any larger chunks, without mushing the tuna too much.

Add the tuna mixture to the bowl with the pasta. Add the feta and rocket and gently toss to combine. Season to taste with salt and a generous amount of pepper. Serve warm or cold, as desired, with lemon wedges for squeezing.

penne with chilli meatballs and crisp garlic bread

Sure, nothing could replace nonna's home-made meatball recipe, but not many of us have a live-in Italian grandmother! So here is what you do: get your hands on some good-quality beef sausages and just squeeze out the filling into walnut-sized balls. Make a very simple tomato sauce and, while it is sizzling away, throw the meatballs into the hot sauce to cook. Working with haste, all this takes about 10, maybe 15 minutes max and the results are delicious.

2 tablespoons olive oil

1 onion, chopped

2 garlic cloves, crushed

2 x 400-g tins chopped tomatoes

1 tablespoon tomato purée

½ teaspoon caster sugar

½ teaspoon dried chilli flakes

400 g skinless beef sausages or plain beef sausages

400 g dried penne, or other pasta shape

freshly grated Parmesan cheese, to serve

sea salt and freshly ground black pepper

garlic bread:

1 baguette

4 tablespoons unsalted butter, softened

3 garlic cloves, crushed

1 tablespoon finely chopped fresh flat leaf parsley

Serves 4

Heat the oil in a frying pan set over high heat. Add the onion and garlic and cook, stirring, for 2–3 minutes, until softened and starting to turn golden.

Add the tomatoes, tomato purée, sugar, chilli flakes and 125 ml water and bring to the boil. Reduce the heat to a simmer.

Using slightly wet hands, squeeze the filling out of the sausage casings, if necessary, and shape into walnut-sized balls. Add these to the tomato sauce. Simmer the meatballs in the sauce for 5 minutes, shaking the pan often to move the meatballs around so that they cook evenly.

Bring a large saucepan of lightly salted water to the boil and cook the penne for 8–10 minutes, until tender.

Meanwhile, to make the garlic bread, preheat the oven to 170°C (325°F) Gas 3. Cut the baguette into 4 equal portions, then cut it in half through the centre. Combine the butter, garlic and parsley in a small bowl and add a little salt. Spread the mixture on the cut side of the baguette, wrap in foil and bake in the preheated oven for about 10 minutes.

Drain the pasta well and return it to the warm pan. Season the meatball sauce to taste with salt and pepper. Spoon the pasta onto serving plates and top with meatballs. Sprinkle with grated Parmesan and serve with the warm garlic bread on the side.

spicy sausage and pepper pizza with rocket salad

Do avoid those thick and doughy frozen pizza bases. I like to use the really good-quality, 'authentic', organic, stonebaked, thin and crispy bases that are now available from larger supermarkets. All of the topping ingredients can be sourced from one good deli counter. If you need a vegetarian alternative, simply substitute the sausages with marinated, chargrilled artichoke hearts. This is delicious washed down with an ice-cold beer.

125 ml passata (sieved tomatoes)

2 x 22-cm good-quality, thin and crispy, ready-made pizza bases

2 spicy Italian sausages, thinly sliced

2 balls of fresh mozzarella cheese

2 tablespoons pickled jalapeño slices

1 large roasted or chargrilled red pepper in oil, thinly sliced

rocket salad:

4 large handfuls of wild rocket

1 tablespoon olive oil

2 teaspoons red wine vinegar

sea salt and freshly ground black pepper

Serves 4

Preheat the oven to 220°C (425°F) Gas 7.

Spread the passata over the pizza bases and randomly top with the sausages, mozzarella, jalapeño and red pepper.

Bake in the preheated oven for about 15 minutes, until the pizza bases are golden and the sausage has cooked through.

While the pizzas are cooking, prepare the salad. Put the rocket in a large bowl. Put the oil and vinegar in a small bowl and whisk with a fork to combine. Pour over the rocket and toss well. Season to taste with salt and pepper.

Serve the rocket salad on the side or arrange in small mounds in the centre of each pizza. Serve immediately.

linguine with garlic and chilli clams

You will always see this on the menu at restaurants in Italy, especially in the coastal towns where good seafood is fresh, plentiful and inexpensive. It is one of those restaurant meals you can successfully cook at home in a flash. As always with dishes that have very few ingredients, the quality and freshness of those ingredients is key. Buy your clams as fresh as possible and try to find small ones – I find they are sweeter and more tender than the larger varieties. Do use a good, fruity extra virgin olive oil too – you will taste the difference.

1 kg fresh clams, well scrubbed

400 g dried linguine or spaghetti

65 ml extra virgin olive oil

3 garlic cloves, roughly chopped

2 large red chillies, deseeded and chopped

65 ml dry white wine

a handful of fresh flat leaf parsley leaves, roughly chopped

sea salt and freshly ground black pepper

crusty bread, to serve

Serves 4

Tap each clam lightly on the work surface and discard any that won't close.

Bring a large saucepan of lightly salted water to the boil and cook the pasta for 8–10 minutes, until tender. Return to the warm pan.

Meanwhile, heat the oil in a large saucepan set over medium heat. Add the garlic and chillies and cook until the garlic just starts to sizzle, flavouring the oil without burning. Increase the heat to high, add the wine and cook until it boils and has reduced by half.

Add the clams, cover the pan tightly and cook for 3–4 minutes, shaking the pan to encourage the clams to open. Discard any clams that don't open.

Add the pasta to the pan, toss to combine and season to taste with salt and pepper. Stir in the parsley and serve immediately with good crusty bread on the side for mopping up the juices.

lemon harissa chicken with oven-roasted vegetables

North African flavours are exciting and exotic, but the cooking techniques are often simple and quick. Preserved lemons are used extensively in Moroccan cooking and are whole lemons packed in jars with salt. The interesting thing is that you eat only the rind, which contains the essential flavour of the lemon, rather than the flesh. They are available from specialist retailers and worth tracking down. Any leftover chicken makes a good sandwich filling with some mayonnaise and rocket, but don't assume there will be any leftovers!

a large handful each of fresh coriander, mint and flat leaf parsley leaves

2 garlic cloves

3 small red chillies, deseeded

½ teaspoon ground cumin

1 tablespoon chopped preserved lemon

4 tablespoons olive oil

6 chicken thigh fillets, halved

1 medium aubergine, cut into large cubes

2 courgettes, thickly sliced

1 small red pepper, quartered and deseeded

1 red onion, cut into thin wedges

2 tablespoons freshly squeezed lemon juice

sea salt and freshly ground black pepper

couscous, to serve (optional)

lemon wedges, to serve

Serves 4

Preheat the oven to 220°C (425°F) Gas 7.

Put the herbs, garlic, chillies, cumin, preserved lemon, 1 tablespoon of the oil and a little salt and pepper in a food processor and process until finely chopped. Put the chicken in a non-reactive bowl, add the herb mixture and toss to coat the chicken. Cover and refrigerate while cooking the vegetables.

Put 2 tablespoons of the olive oil in a roasting tin and put it in the oven for 10 minutes to heat up.

Put the aubergine, courgettes, red pepper and onion in the hot roasting tin and season well with salt and pepper. Cook in the preheated oven for 40 minutes, shaking the pan and turning the vegetables after about 20 minutes. Remove from the oven and cover with foil to keep warm while you cook the chicken.

Heat the remaining oil in a frying pan set over medium heat. Put the chicken in the pan and reserve the marinade in the bowl. Cook the chicken for 7–8 minutes, until a golden crust forms, spooning the reserved marinade over the top. Turn over and cook for 5 minutes, until cooked through. Pour the lemon juice over the chicken and turn the chicken over in the pan.

Arrange the vegetables and chicken on a serving platter. Serve with couscous, if liked, and lemon wedges on the side for squeezing.

roast chicken and minted tabbouleh salad

Thankfully, free-range, organic rotisserie chickens are now readily available in larger supermarkets. They are on my top ten list of great time-savers. Shred the flesh and use in soups, pie fillings (see Chicken Pot Pies on page 51) or in a substantial main course salad, as here.

130 g bulghur wheat

1 rotisserie chicken

a large handful each of fresh mint, flat leaf parsley and coriander leaves, finely chopped

3 roma tomatoes, halved

2 cucumbers chopped

2 Little Gem lettuces, washed and leaves separated

2 tablespoons freshly squeezed lemon juice

65 ml olive oil

sea salt and freshly ground black pepper

wholemeal pitta breads, to serve

Serves 4

Put the bulghur wheat in a heatproof bowl and pour in 185 ml boiling water. Cover and set aside for 15 minutes. Stir well to fluff the grains up and tip into a larger bowl.

Shred the meat and skin, if liked, of the chicken and put it in the bowl with the bulghur wheat. Add the herbs, tomatoes, cucumber and lettuce leaves.

Put the lemon juice and olive oil in a small bowl and whisk with a fork to combine. Pour over the salad. Season to taste with salt and pepper and toss to combine all the ingredients. Serve immediately with warmed wholemeal pitta breads on the side.

Keralan prawn curry

Here is a speedy curry that's typical of what you'd eat in southern India. Coconuts grow in abundance in Kerala and so grated coconut and coconut milk are widely used in the region's curries. Because of the long coastline, lots of seafood is used too, which means light dishes that require very little cooking time – perfect for the stressed midweek cook!

2 onions, chopped

4 garlic cloves, chopped

2 tablespoons butter

16 large raw prawns, peeled and deveined

2 large green chillies, thinly sliced

4 tomatoes, roughly chopped

2 tablespoons white wine vinegar

5-cm piece of fresh ginger, peeled and cut into matchsticks

60 ml coconut cream

a handful of fresh coriander leaves, chopped

warmed naan bread, to serve

Serves 4

Put the onions and garlic in a food processor and process until very finely chopped. Set aside.

Heat the butter in a frying pan set over medium heat. When the butter is sizzling, add the prawns and cook for just 1 minute on each side, until pale pink and curled. Remove from the pan.

Add the onion mixture and cook for 5 minutes, stirring often, until softened and golden. Add the chillies, tomatoes, vinegar, ginger and 125 ml water. Bring to the boil and cook for 5 minutes, until thickened. Add the prawns and cook for 2–3 minutes, until they are cooked through. Stir in the coconut cream and coriander and gently cook for 1 minute just to heat through. Serve with warmed naan bread on the side.

See photograph on page 94.

Thai-style golden prawn noodle salad

Thai flavours are so bright and fresh and the ingredients are now readily available. While this is a great outdoor summer entertaining dish, it is so vibrant and cheery that it may be served up in colder months to add a bit of colour to gloomy days.

200 g dried vermicelli rice noodles
1 tablespoon ground turmeric
500 g large cooked prawns, peeled and deveined
1 red pepper, deseeded and thinly sliced
3 spring onions, thinly sliced on the angle
1 large green chilli, thinly sliced
a small bunch of fresh coriander, leaves and some stalks roughly chopped and a few small sprigs reserved to garnish
3 tablespoons Thai fish sauce
2 tablespoons freshly squeezed lime juice
1 teaspoon caster sugar

Serves 4

Put the noodles in a large, heatproof bowl.

Put 1.5 litres water in a saucepan and set over high heat. Add the turmeric and bring to the boil. As soon as the water boils, pour it over the noodles and leave for 5–6 minutes, until the noodles are cooked. Rinse and drain well.

Transfer the noodles to a separate bowl with the prawns, red pepper, spring onions, chilli and coriander.

Put the fish sauce, lime juice and sugar in a small bowl and whisk with a fork to combine. Pour over the noodles. Sprinkle with the coriander sprigs and serve immediately.

See photograph on page 95.

baked chipolatas in tomato and basil sauce on soft polenta

This is perfect comfort food in a flash. If you're not a fan of polenta, you could serve these sausages with creamy mashed potatoes instead. Any leftovers make an ideal winter brunch treat – top with a poached egg and serve with plenty of buttered toast.

8 good-quality chipolata sausages, pricked with a fork
1 red onion, peeled and cut into thin wedges
4 garlic cloves, roughly chopped
2 tablespoons olive oil
400-g tin chopped tomatoes
a handful of fresh basil leaves
sea salt and freshly ground black pepper
freshly grated Parmesan cheese, to serve

soft polenta:
500 ml full-fat milk
200 g instant polenta
50 g butter, cut into cubes
50 g Parmesan cheese, finely grated

Serves 4

Preheat the oven to 220°C (425°F) Gas 7.

Put the sausages, onion and garlic in a roasting tin and pour over the olive oil. Season well with salt and pepper and cook in the preheated oven for 15 minutes.

Remove the roasting tin from the oven, stir the sausage mixture and pour over the tinned tomatoes. Return to the oven for a further 20 minutes.

Chop some of the basil leaves and stir them into the sausage mixture, reserving a few to garnish.

To make the polenta, put the milk and 500 ml water in a large saucepan and bring to the boil. Pour the polenta into the boiling liquid in a steady stream and whisk constantly, until combined. Reduce the heat to low and beat with a wooden spoon for about 2–3 minutes. Stir in the butter and grated Parmesan.

Spoon the soft polenta onto a large serving platter and top with the sausages and sauce. Sprinkle with the reserved basil leaves and serve immediately with grated Parmesan on the side.

za'atar salmon with lentil salad

This blend of thyme, oregano and sesame seeds is called za'atar. Enjoyed all over the Middle East, Morocco and Egypt, it is generally used as a dry condiment to sprinkle on bread dipped in olive oil. This style of cooking is perfect for last-minute entertaining, as with a pinch or two of storecupboard staples you can bring everyday ingredients to life.

65 ml olive oil
2 tablespoons freshly squeezed lemon juice
1 teaspoon dried thyme
1 teaspoon dried wild oregano
1 tablespoon sesame seeds
4 salmon fillets, about 180 g each
sea salt and freshly ground black pepper

lentil salad:
1 aubergine, cut into small cubes
250 g cherry tomatoes
1 red onion, thinly sliced
2 garlic cloves, chopped
1 teaspoon ground cumin
400-g tin cooked lentils, drained
1 tablespoon red wine vinegar
a large handful of fresh coriander leaves, chopped

a baking tray lined with baking paper

Serves 4

Preheat the oven to 220°C (425°F) Gas 7.

Put half of the olive oil, lemon juice, thyme, oregano and sesame seeds in a large non-reactive bowl and season with salt and pepper. Whisk with a fork to combine. Add the salmon and toss to coat. Set aside to allow the flavours to develop while you make the salad.

Heat the remaining olive oil in a frying pan set over high heat. Add the aubergine and cook for 2–3 minutes, turning often, until golden. Add the tomatoes, onion and garlic and cook for 2 minutes, shaking the pan so that the tomatoes soften. Add the cumin, lentils and vinegar and remove from the heat. Stir in the coriander.

Put the salmon on the prepared baking tray and cook in the preheated oven for 10 minutes, until just cooked through. Spoon the lentil salad onto a large platter and arrange the salmon on top. Serve immediately.

iced mint tea

This refreshing iced tea makes the perfect companion to the spicy flavours of the Za'atar Salmon (see left).

2 teaspoons green tea leaves
3 tablespoons caster sugar
a handful of fresh mint sprigs
125 ml vodka (optional)
soda water, to top up
ice cubes, to serve

4 serving glasses (preferably ornate Moroccan tea glasses)

Serves 4

Put the green tea and sugar in a small saucepan with 250 ml water. Bring to the boil, reduce the heat and cook for 5 minutes, until the liquid is slightly syrupy and dark from the tea. Pour into a jug and refrigerate until well chilled.

Put ice cubes in 4 serving glasses. Put a few sprigs of mint in each and divide the vodka between the glasses.

Pour over the green tea mixture and top up with soda water. Serve immediately.

pine-lime fizz

A fresh and zesty drink that's perfect served with the Chilli Salt Squid on page 27.

2 tablespoons lime syrup
125 ml vodka
250 ml pineapple juice
125 ml white rum (optional)
1 lime, thinly sliced
750 ml soda water, chilled
ice cubes, to serve

Serves 4

Combine the lime syrup, vodka, pineapple juice and rum in a jug. Refrigerate until chilled.

Put the ice cubes and lime slices in serving glasses. Add the pineapple mixture and top up with soda water. Serve immediately.

See photograph on page 26.

chic eats

foraged mushroom risotto

The mushrooms you see at farmers' markets will either be cultivated or wild. Wild mushroom varieties are foraged – that is to say, they are hand-picked by experts, enthusiasts and fanatics alike called mycologists. They are an exotic treat, but it is notoriously tricky for the untrained eye to determine safe-to-eat varieties, so I for one am more than happy to pay a bit extra to avoid being poisoned!

20 g dried porcini mushrooms

2 tablespoons olive oil

3 tablespoons butter

500 g mixed foraged or wild mushrooms, roughly chopped

1 litre vegetable stock

125 ml dry white wine

1 onion, chopped

2 garlic cloves, finely chopped

330 g arborio (risotto) rice

100 g Parmesan cheese, finely grated

a small handful of fresh flat leaf parsley, finely chopped

sea salt and freshly ground black pepper

Serves 4

Put the dried mushrooms in a heatproof bowl and pour in 500 ml boiling water. Let soak for 30 minutes, then drain, reserving 250 ml of the liquid. Finely chop the mushrooms and set aside.

Heat 1 tablespoon of the oil and half of the butter in a heavy-based saucepan set over medium heat. Add the fresh mushrooms and cook for 8–10 minutes, stirring often, until softened and aromatic. Remove from the pan and set aside.

Put the reserved mushroom liquid in a separate saucepan. Add the stock and wine and set over low heat.

Add the remaining oil and butter to the mushroom pan. Add the onion and garlic and cook for 2–3 minutes, until softened. Add the rice and stir for 1 minute, until the rice is glossy. Reduce the heat to low, add about 125 ml of the hot stock mixture and cook, stirring often, until the stock has been absorbed. Repeat until all the stock has been used and the rice is tender yet still firm to the bite.

Stir in half of the Parmesan and season to taste with salt and pepper. Serve with the remaining Parmesan sprinkled over the top along with the chopped parsley.

truffled egg linguine

This posh-sounding but surprisingly simple recipe calls for the finest ingredients: organic hen's eggs, good-quality Parmesan and pecorino cheeses and truffle oil. Some die hard purists are set against the use of truffle oil in cooking, but truffles are next to impossible to source where I come from, so I enjoy this luxury treat, which, when stored in a cool, dry place away from direct sunlight, will keep for ages. Try to source some good fresh pasta for this and taste the difference. As well as being fancy, this is great fun – toss it on the plate in front of your guests for a bit of restaurant-style cabaret at home.

125 ml single cream
1 tablespoon butter
4 very fresh eggs
2 tablespoons olive oil
300 g fresh linguine
1 teaspoon truffle oil
50 g pecorino cheese, finely grated
50 g Parmesan cheese, finely grated
sea salt

Serves 4

Bring a large saucepan of lightly salted water to the boil.

Put the cream and butter in a small saucepan and set over low heat.

Put the olive oil in a large, non-stick frying pan set over medium heat. Crack one egg at a time into the pan. Alternatively, to help prevent the yolks from breaking, crack each one into a small jug, then pour into the pan. Cook the eggs so that the whites just start to turn and firm up around the edge, then slide onto a plate.

Cook the pasta in the boiling water for 2–3 minutes, until it rises to the top – fresh pasta cooks much faster than dried. Working quickly, as you want the pasta to be as hot as possible, drain well and return to the warm pan. Pour in the cream mixture. Gently toss to combine, then divide the pasta between 4 serving plates. Put an egg on top of each one and drizzle truffle oil over each egg. Sprinkle a quarter of the cheeses over each one.

Use a spoon and fork to toss all the ingredients together so that the yolk combines with the hot pasta and thickens the sauce, and the egg whites are roughly chopped and combined with the linguine. Eat immediately.

soft goat's cheese and fennel tart

I know the idea of making your own pastry can be a little daunting – I prefer to make my own shortcrust, but don't mind using ready-made puff pastry. That said, this pastry recipe is so unintimidating that you should give it a go. It has just two ingredients and check out the method – NO ROLLING! Make the pastry in the food processor, form it into a ball, then press it directly into the tart tin. The whole tart can be made well in advance and served at room temperature with a peppery wild rocket salad.

4 fennel bulbs, with feathery tops intact

2 tablespoons olive oil

200 g soft goat's cheese, roughly crumbled

65 g walnut halves

3 eggs

185 ml single cream

1 tablespoon snipped fresh chives

sea salt and freshly ground black pepper

dressed wild rocket leaves, to serve

pastry:

170 g plain flour

80 g butter, cut into cubes and chilled

a loose-bottomed tart tin, about 24 cm diameter, lightly greased

baking weights (optional)

Serves 6–8

Preheat the oven to 180°C (350°F) Gas 4.

To make the pastry, put the flour in a food processor. With the motor running, add the butter and process until the mixture resembles coarse breadcrumbs. Add 2–3 tablespoons chilled water and process until the dough just starts to come together. Tip the dough out onto a lightly-floured work surface and use your hands to form it into a ball, gathering all the smaller pieces together. Do not knead it too much.

Put the dough in the centre of the prepared tart tin and use your thumbs to press it down into the tin, working outwards from the centre and making sure the pastry comes up over the side of the tin. Prick the base all over with the tines of a fork. Cover the pastry with a sheet of baking paper and fill with baking weights, dried beans or rice. Bake in the preheated oven for about 20 minutes, until the pastry looks dry and golden.

Remove the feathery tops from the fennel. Chop them finely to give about 3 tablespoons and set aside. Cut the fennel bulbs into thin wedges. Put them in a roasting tin, add the olive oil and season well with salt and pepper. Cook in the still-hot oven for 40 minutes, turning after 20 minutes, until golden and tender. Let cool to room temperature.

Arrange the fennel in the tart case and scatter the cheese and walnuts randomly over and in between the pieces of fennel. Put the eggs, cream and chives in a jug or bowl. Whisk with a fork to combine, season well and pour over the fennel. Bake in the still-hot oven for about 45 minutes, until puffed and golden on top. Serve the tart warm or at room temperature with a dressed rocket salad on the side.

spiced tomatoes with couscous salad

This recipe was just made for eating outdoors on a summer's afternoon. Rethink your attitude to tomatoes – they don't have to be red to be ripe! Look for heirloom varieties that come in all different colours. Firm green- and yellow-tinged varieties hold their shape well and are perfect for pan-frying.

1 teaspoon ground cumin
1 teaspoon smoked paprika (pimentón)
½ teaspoon chilli powder
1 teaspoon sea salt
3 tablespoons olive oil
4 large ripe heirloom tomatoes, thickly sliced
freshly ground black pepper

couscous salad:
250 g couscous
1 tablespoon butter
1 cucumber, peeled, deseeded and diced
2 spring onions, thinly sliced
a handful each of fresh flat leaf parsley and mint, chopped
2 tablespoons olive oil
100 g feta cheese, crumbled
80 g almonds, preferably smoked

Serves 4

To make the couscous salad, put the couscous and butter in a heatproof bowl. Add 250 ml boiling water, stir a few times and cover. Let sit for 10 minutes. Using a fork, fluff the couscous. Cover and let sit for a further 5 minutes. Tip into a large bowl. When cool enough to handle, use your fingers to fluff and separate the grains. Add the cucumber, spring onions, parsley, mint and olive oil and toss to combine. Add the feta and almonds just before serving.

Combine the cumin, paprika, chilli powder, salt and a few grinds of black pepper in a small bowl. Heat the oil in a frying pan set over high heat. Sprinkle half of the spice mixture over one side of the tomatoes and add to the frying pan, spice-side down. Cook for 2 minutes. Sprinkle the remaining mixture on the uncooked side of the tomatoes, turn over and cook for a further 2 minutes.

Arrange the couscous salad on a serving platter. Lay the tomatoes on top and serve immediately.

See photograph on page 1.

stuffed giant mushrooms with feta and herbs

Look out for pine mushrooms in the autumn. They will be foraged and hand-picked by specialists. I like them cooked whole with as little fuss as possible. Their flavour is best appreciated if they are left to sit for a short while and served warm rather than hot.

8 very large mushrooms, stalks removed
100 g feta cheese, grated
40 g blanched almonds, roughly chopped
50 g stale white breadcrumbs
1 tablespoon chopped fresh flat leaf parsley
1 tablespoon snipped fresh chives
2 teaspoons olive oil
1 tablespoon chilled butter, finely cubed, plus 2 tablespoons extra
6 baby courgettes, halved lengthways
100 g fine green beans, trimmed
4 small leeks, thinly sliced
65 ml dry white wine
freshly squeezed lemon juice, to taste
sea salt and freshly ground black pepper

an ovenproof baking dish, lightly oiled

Serves 4

Preheat the oven to 170°C (325°F) Gas 3.

Sit the mushrooms, gill-side up, in the prepared baking dish. Put the feta, almonds, breadcrumbs and herbs in a bowl and use your fingers to quickly combine. Stir in the olive oil. Spoon the mixture into the mushrooms and press down gently. Dot the cubed butter over the top. Bake in the preheated oven for about 40–45 minutes, until the mushrooms are really soft and the tops golden.

Meanwhile, bring a saucepan of lightly salted water to the boil. Add the courgettes and beans to the water and cook for 1 minute. Drain well and set aside. About 15 minutes before the mushrooms are cooked, heat the extra butter in a frying pan set over high heat. Add the leeks and cook for 2 minutes, stirring until softened. Add the courgettes and beans and cook for 2–3 minutes, until tender. Add the wine and cook for 1 minute, until almost all of it has evaporated. Add a squeeze of lemon juice and season well. Arrange the vegetables on a serving plate and sit the mushrooms on top.

Spanish bouillabaisse

As with any good seafood recipe, this dish is all about the quality of the produce. The soup base can be made a few hours in advance, up to the point where you've added and cooked the rice. All you need to do is reheat the soup and add the fresh seafood when you are ready to serve it to your guests.

2 tablespoons olive oil

1 red onion, chopped

2 garlic cloves, chopped

1 chorizo sausage, finely chopped

1 carrot, grated

1 teaspoon finely grated orange zest

2 litres fish stock

400-g tin chopped tomatoes

55 g arborio (risotto) rice

200 g skinless salmon fillet, cut into 2-cm pieces

1 cleaned squid tube, thinly sliced

12 raw prawns, peeled and deveined

a handful of fresh flat leaf parsley leaves, finely chopped

sea salt and freshly ground black pepper

Serves 4

Heat the oil in a large saucepan set over medium heat. Add the onion, garlic, chorizo, carrot and orange zest and cook for about 10 minutes, stirring often, until softened and aromatic. Add the fish stock, tomatoes and rice and bring to the boil. Reduce the heat to medium and let simmer, uncovered, for about 15 minutes, until the soup thickens and the rice is cooked.

Add the prepared salmon, squid and prawns, cover and cook for 2–3 minutes, until the seafood is all cooked through and the prawns are pink. Season to taste with salt and pepper and stir in the parsley. Ladle into serving bowls and serve immediately.

baked salmon with chilli and fresh herbs

Most of us probably don't own a fish steamer, but fear not. The trick here is to wrap the salmon in damp newspaper and bake it in the oven – it keeps the fish moist and works perfectly!

1 large salmon fillet, about 700–750 g

a handful of fresh flat leaf parsley leaves, roughly chopped

a handful of fresh mint leaves, roughly chopped

2 tablespoons roughly chopped fresh dill

1 large red chilli, thinly sliced

2 spring onions, very thinly sliced on the diagonal

2 tablespoons freshly squeezed lemon juice

3 tablespoons olive oil

sea salt and freshly ground black pepper

Serves 4

Preheat the oven to 220°C (425°F) Gas 7.

Wet some newspaper, enough to cover the base of a roasting tin. Sit a piece of baking paper on the newspaper and put the fish fillet on the paper. Scatter the herbs, chilli and spring onions over the fish. Put the lemon juice and olive oil in a small bowl or jug and whisk with a fork to combine. Pour over the fish. Season with salt and pepper and lay another sheet of baking paper loosely on top. Wet some more newspaper and lay it over the roasting tin to cover.

Cook in the preheated oven for about 10 minutes, until the fish is slightly rare in the centre. Remove from the oven, but let the fish sit in the paper for 5 minutes to continue steaming. Serve with boiled new potatoes, if liked.

See photograph on page 112.

spaghetti with 'fruits of the sea'

Where I live, some fishmongers sell what they call 'marinara mix', but I think it's a lazy way to buy seafood. If you hand-pick exactly what you need for your dish, you'll be rewarded. That way you can choose prime ingredients such as in-season scallops, plump, sweet mussels and line-caught fish. Your hand-picked selection will be fresher and less pricey.

3 tablespoons olive oil
2 garlic cloves, roughly chopped
1 onion, finely chopped
2 fresh or dried bay leaves
300 g cherry tomatoes
½ teaspoon caster sugar
125 ml sweet white wine
500 g fresh mussels
16 medium raw prawns, peeled and deveined
12 shelled and cleaned scallops
300 g monkfish fillet, cut into 3-cm pieces
400 g dried spaghetti
sea salt and freshly ground black pepper

Serves 4

Heat the oil in a large frying pan set over high heat. Add the garlic, onion, bay leaves and a pinch of salt. Cook for 5 minutes, stirring often. Add the tomatoes, sugar and wine. Bring the mixture to the boil for 2–3 minutes, until the tomatoes have softened. Add 250 ml water to the pan and boil for 5 minutes, gently pressing on the tomatoes so that they split. Remove the pan from the heat.

Scrub the mussels well, knock off any barnacles and pull off the beards. Discard any broken mussels and any that won't close when they are tapped on the work surface. Drain in a colander and set aside until needed.

Bring a large saucepan of water to the boil. Add the prawns, scallops and monkfish and poach in the water for 2 minutes. Remove with a slotted spoon and add to the tomato sauce. Return the water to the boil. Add the spaghetti and cook for 10–12 minutes, until tender yet still firm to the bite. Drain well.

Bring the tomato sauce back to high heat. Add the mussels, cover and cook for 4–5 minutes, until the mussels open. Discard any that don't open. Add the pasta and gently toss to combine with the sauce. Season to taste with salt and pepper and serve immediately.

See photograph on page 113.

snapper pie

This fish pie is very different to the béchamel sauce recipes you may have cooked before. The delicious sweet onion sauce is based on the French classic 'soubise'. Be ready to give the recipe to your guests!

1 tablespoon olive oil
1 tablespoon butter
900 g white onions, thinly sliced
2 fresh or dry bay leaves
375 ml fish stock
500 ml single cream
1 sheet ready-rolled puff pastry, defrosted if frozen
800 g red snapper fillet, cut into bite-sized pieces
milk, for glazing
sea salt and freshly ground black pepper

4 individual ovenproof baking dishes, about 10–15 cm diameter

Serves 4

Heat the olive oil and butter in a heavy-based saucepan set over medium heat. Add the onions and bay leaves and stir well to break up the onions. Cover and cook for about 30 minutes, stirring often so that the onions sweat and soften. Remove the lid and increase the heat to high. Cook for a further 10 minutes, stirring occasionally so that the onions do not catch and are a pale caramel colour.

Add the fish stock, bring to the boil and cook until the liquid has reduced by half. Reduce the heat to medium and add the cream. Cook for about 15 minutes, stirring constantly. Remove from the heat and let cool. Remove the bay leaves and blend the sauce in a food processor until smooth. Set aside until needed.

Preheat the oven to 220°C (425°F) Gas 7.

Lightly flour a work surface. Roll the pastry out to a thickness of about 2–3 mm. Cut 4 circles from the pastry, using an upturned baking dish as a template.

Spoon half of the onion sauce into each of the baking dishes. Arrange a quarter of the fish pieces on top, then spoon over the remaining sauce. Repeat to fill 4 pies. Cover each pie with a pastry circle and press around the edges with the tines of a fork to seal. Use a sharp knife to make 2–3 small incisions in the pastry to let the steam escape. Brush the top of each with a little milk to glaze and bake in the preheated oven for 20–25 minutes, until golden and puffed. Serve with a watercress salad, if liked.

brined roast chicken with a ham and fresh sage stuffing

Brining is the most basic of marinades. Prepared and cooked this way, your roast chicken will be full of flavour and truly memorable. If you are pressed for time, you can leave out the brining, but I strongly recommend that you don't. If you are brining, do bear in mind that the chicken will need to be in the liquid for at least three hours and removed from the brine one hour before cooking.

3 tablespoons sea salt

2 tablespoons granulated white sugar

2 fresh or dried bay leaves

1 roasting chicken, about 1.8 kg

2 tablespoons butter, softened

ham and fresh sage stuffing:

5 slices of stale white bread, crusts removed, roughly torn

2 tablespoons butter

1 small onion, finely chopped

2 garlic cloves, chopped

100 g smoked ham, finely chopped

2 tablespoons finely chopped fresh sage

1 egg

a large non-reactive bowl, big enough to take the chicken and 3 litres liquid

kitchen string

Serves 4

Put the salt, sugar and bay leaves in a very large saucepan with 3 litres water. Bring to the boil, stirring a few times until the salt and sugar have dissolved, then remove from the heat. Let cool to room temperature. Sit the chicken in the non-reactive bowl and pour in the liquid so that the chicken is fully immersed. Cover and put somewhere cold to sit for 3–6 hours.

To make the stuffing, put the bread in a food processor and process to make coarse crumbs. Tip the crumbs into a bowl and set aside.

Heat the butter in a saucepan set over medium heat and cook the onion for 5 minutes, until softened. Add the garlic, ham and sage and stir-fry for 1 minute. Add the mixture to the crumbs with the egg and use your hands to combine well.

Remove the chicken from the brine 1 hour before cooking.

Preheat the oven to 170°C (325°F) Gas 3.

Spoon the stuffing into the cavity of the chicken and tie the legs firmly together with kitchen string.

Put the chicken in a roasting tin and rub the butter over the top side. Roast in the preheated oven for 1½ hours, until the skin of the chicken is golden and the meat is cooked through. To test, insert a skewer into the chicken where the leg joins the breast – if the juices run clear, it is cooked. Let the chicken rest in a warm place for 30 minutes before carving. Serve with roasted root vegetables and sautéed green beans, if liked.

roast turkey breast with olive salsa verde

Lean turkey meat pairs very well with strong flavours, so it works perfectly here with a sharp and tangy salsa. While I would generally encourage you to do plenty of preparation ahead of time when entertaining, here the salsa is definitely best made as close to the time that you intend to eat it as possible. It will oxidize very quickly and lose much of its vibrant fresh taste.

1 turkey breast, about 1.8 kg, skin-on
2 tablespoons light olive oil
2 teaspoons smoked paprika (pimentón)
8 slices of prosciutto
sea salt and freshly ground black pepper

olive salsa verde:
100 g stoned green olives
3 baby gherkins (cornichons)
a bunch of fresh flat leaf parsley leaves
a large handful of fresh mint leaves
2 garlic cloves, chopped
3 anchovy fillets in olive oil, drained
3 tablespoons freshly squeezed lemon juice
125 ml olive oil

a large flameproof roasting tin

Serves 6–8

Preheat the oven to 180°C (350°F) Gas 4.

Wash the turkey and pat it dry. Season the skin well with salt and pepper. Heat the light olive oil in a roasting tin set over high heat and cook the turkey, skin-side down, for 5 minutes, until the skin is golden. Remove the turkey from the tin, leaving any residual oil in the tin. Sprinkle the paprika over the skin. Lay the prosciutto slices side by side and slightly overlapping over the entire skin side of the turkey, tucking them in underneath the breast.

Return the turkey to the roasting tin, sitting it skin-side up. Cook in the preheated oven for 1¼ hours, basting occasionally with the pan juices. Increase the heat to 220°C (425°F) Gas 7 and cook for a further 10–15 minutes so that the prosciutto and skin is very crisp. Remove, and lightly cover in foil.

To make the olive salsa verde, put all of the ingredients in a food processor and process until well combined and coarsely chopped, but do not overprocess.

Carve the turkey into thick slices. To serve, plate the turkey and spoon the olive salsa verde over the top. Serve with roast new potatoes and sautéed baby carrots, if liked.

roast ducklings with orange and ginger pilaf

While many of us love duck, most of us would admit to being just a little bit afraid of cooking it at home. But fear not, you can't really go wrong with this recipe! The ducklings are initially slow-cooked, rendering out much of the fat, and then blasted in a hot oven for the remainder of the cooking time, which produces lovely crisp skin. And while that is happening, you'll have plenty of time to get the delicious orange and ginger pilaf ready.

2 ducklings, about 1.5–1.6 kg each

2 oranges

10-cm piece of fresh ginger

2 tablespoons olive oil

1 tablespoon butter

6 shallots, thinly sliced

2 fresh or dried bay leaves

2 garlic cloves, chopped

400 g basmati rice

500 ml chicken stock

a generous pinch of saffron threads

sea salt

Serves 4

Preheat the oven to 130°C (250°F) Gas ½.

Trim the fatty area around the parson's nose (the tail end of the ducklings). Tuck the neck and wings underneath the bird. Using a skewer, pierce the skin all over without piercing the flesh.

Finely grate the zest of one of the oranges and set aside. Cut both oranges in half. Squeeze both oranges to give 125 ml juice. Put 2 of the halves in the cavity of each duckling. Thinly slice half of the ginger and put it in with the oranges. Finely grate the remaining ginger and set aside.

Rub the ducklings all over with salt. Sit them on a cooking rack set over a deep roasting tin to collect the rendered fat. Cook in the preheated oven for 2 hours, basting with the duck fat every 30 minutes or so.

Increase the oven temperature to 220°C (425°F) Gas 7 and pour 250 ml water into the roasting tin. Return the ducklings to the oven and cook for a further 20–30 minutes, until the skin is golden and crisp. Remove from the oven and let rest for 30 minutes before carving into thick slices.

Meanwhile, to make the pilaf, heat the oil and butter in a large heavy-based saucepan set over medium heat. Add the orange zest, grated ginger, shallots, bay leaves and garlic and cook, stirring, for 2–3 minutes, until softened.

Add the rice and cook for 2 minutes, stirring to combine the rice with the other ingredients. Add the stock, orange juice and saffron. Briskly stir a few times to remove any stuck-on bits from the bottom of the pan and bring to the boil. Cover and cook over low heat for 20 minutes. Remove from the heat and stir a few times. Set the cooked rice aside.

To serve, plate a few slices of the duckling with the pilaf on the side and a watercress salad, if liked.

paprika osso buco
with minted pea pasta

You'll no doubt be familiar with the classic Milanese dish of osso buco. It comprises veal shanks braised in stock and white wine with onions, carrots, celery, garlic, anchovies and lemon peel. But osso buco, when translated from the Italian, literally means 'bone with a hole' or 'pierced bone' and actually refers to the cut of meat, so you can cook it in any way you like. I have made a version before now with Chinese flavours such as rice wine, soy sauce and ginger and served it with rice and Asian greens. The smoked paprika in this recipe gives the dish a Spanish feel.

4 veal osso buco, about 200 g each

30 g plain flour

3 tablespoons olive oil

2 tablespoons butter

1 onion, chopped

3 garlic cloves, chopped

1 carrot, cut into bite-sized pieces

1 celery stick, chopped

1 tablespoon smoked paprika (pimentón)

2 fresh or dried bay leaves

250 ml dry white wine

400-g tin chopped tomatoes

375 ml chicken stock

a handful of fresh flat leaf parsley, finely chopped

sea salt and freshly ground black pepper

minted pea pasta:

200 g any small dried 'soup' pasta, such as orzo, risi or stelle (as I've used here)

100 g frozen peas

a small handful of fresh mint leaves, finely chopped

2 tablespoons butter

a large, heavy-based flameproof casserole

Serves 4

Put the veal in a bowl with the flour and season well with salt and pepper.

Put 2 tablespoons of the oil and the butter in the casserole and set over medium heat. Shake any excess flour off the veal and add the veal to the pan. Cook for about 5 minutes, turning a few times, until golden all over. Remove from the pan and set aside.

Add the remaining oil to the pan. Add the onion, garlic, carrot and celery and cook for 5 minutes, stirring, until softened. Add the paprika, bay leaves and wine and increase the heat to high. Let boil for about 5 minutes, scraping the bottom of the pan to combine any stuck-on bits, until the liquid has thickened.

Add the tomatoes, stock and half of the parsley. Return the veal to the pan. Bring to the boil, then reduce to low heat. Cover and cook for 1 hour, turning the veal after 30 minutes. Remove the lid and cook for a further 15–20 minutes, until the sauce is thick and the meat tender. Season to taste.

Meanwhile, to make the minted pea pasta, cook the pasta in a large saucepan of lightly salted boiling water for 8 minutes or according to the packet instructions. Add the peas and cook for a further 2 minutes. Drain well and return to the warm pan. Add the mint and butter. Season to taste with salt and pepper.

Serve the osso buco with the minted pea pasta on the side and sprinkled with the remaining parsley.

slow-cooked lamb shanks in red wine with white beans

Lamb shanks have recently became popular again but at one time they were trimmed off and discarded by the butcher. It's great that they are enjoying a revival, as they make easy work of entertaining – you should allow one shank per person, which is simple enough, and the meat is best slow-cooked, which leaves you plenty of time to get on with preparing a dessert. The addition of white beans makes this a rustic, hearty dish – perfect comfort food for hungry guests. Don't forget to allow plenty of time to soak the beans.

100 g dried white beans, such as cannellini or butter beans

4 trimmed lamb shanks, about 400 g each

40 g pancetta, chopped

400-g tin chopped tomatoes

500 ml beef stock

250 ml red wine

2 tablespoons sun-dried tomato paste

1 fresh or dried bay leaf

2 sprigs of fresh thyme

a handful of fresh flat leaf parsley, finely chopped

sea salt and freshly ground black pepper

a large casserole with a tight-fitting lid

Serves 4

Put the white beans in a bowl. Cover with cold water and let soak for 6 hours or overnight. Drain well and set aside.

Preheat the oven to 170ºC (325ºF) Gas 3.

Put the lamb shanks in the casserole. Add the pancetta, tomatoes, stock, red wine, sun-dried tomato paste, bay leaf, thyme and half of the parsley. Season well with salt and pepper, stir to combine and cover tightly.

Cook in the preheated oven for 2 hours. Remove the casserole from the oven, turn the shanks over and add the beans. Re-cover and return the casserole to the oven and cook for a further hour, until the mixture is thick and the lamb is very tender.

To serve, spoon a quarter of the beans into each dish, add a lamb shank and spoon some sauce over the top. Sprinkle with the remaining parsley. Serve with some sautéed green beans, if liked.

shoulder of lamb with oven-roasted veg

Where I come from in Australia, in-season lamb is not expensive, but as I travel more I realise how much the price and availability of quality produce varies from place to place. A shoulder of lamb is generally a cheaper cut all year round, but slow-cooked in this way it's truly delicious and guaranteed to satisfy the hungriest of guests.

1.3–1.5 kg shoulder of lamb, on the bone

500 ml dry white wine

250 ml freshly squeezed lemon juice

3 tablespoons olive oil

4 sprigs of fresh rosemary

2 teaspoons dried oregano, preferably Greek

4 garlic cloves, lightly smashed

1 large courgette, roughly chopped

1 large red onion, cut into thin wedges

1 small yellow pepper, deseeded and thickly sliced

3 waxy potatoes, thickly sliced

1 tablespoon finely chopped dill

a handful of fresh flat leaf parsley leaves, roughly chopped

sea salt and freshly ground black pepper

a large flameproof roasting tin
kitchen string

Serves 4

Put the lamb, skin-side up, in a non-reactive dish. Add the wine, lemon juice, 2 tablespoons of the olive oil, the rosemary, oregano and garlic. Cover and refrigerate overnight.

Remove from the refrigerator 1 hour before cooking and season the skin of the lamb well with salt and pepper.

Preheat the oven to 220°C (425°F) Gas 7.

Remove the lamb from the marinade, reserving 2 tablespoons of the liquid. Roll it firmly and secure with kitchen string.

Put the courgette, onion, yellow pepper and potatoes in a bowl with the reserved marinade and use your hands to toss the vegetables until well coated.

Set a roasting tin over high heat and add the remaining olive oil. Heat until very hot. Add the lamb and cook for 5–6 minutes, turning often, until golden all over. Add the vegetables to the tin and cook for 2–3 minutes, turning the vegetables often. Transfer to the preheated oven and cook for 40 minutes, turning the vegetables after 20 minutes. Transfer the vegetables to a bowl, cover with foil and keep warm until ready to serve.

Reduce the oven temperature to 180°C (350°F) Gas 4. Cook the lamb for a further hour, until the skin is dark and crisp. Remove from the oven and cover tightly with foil. Let rest in a warm place for 20 minutes before carving.

Add the dill and parsley to the warm vegetables and season to taste with salt and pepper.

To serve, plate thick slices of the lamb and serve the vegetables on the side.

roast beef rib-eye with café de Paris butter and asparagus

Said to have originated in Geneva in the 1940s, you will see many versions of this delicious butter. Great with steak, but also lovely melted on a piece of fish, hot from the grill. Some recipes have an ingredients list as long as your arm, but essentially it is softened butter combined with curry powder, anchovies, Worchestershire sauce and some fresh herbs.

750–800 g beef fillet

1 tablespoon sea salt

½ teaspoon freshly ground black pepper

1 tablespoon olive oil

a bunch of white asparagus, trimmed and halved

a bunch of green asparagus, trimmed and halved

2 tablespoons butter

café de Paris butter:

1 tablespoon mild mustard

2 teaspoons Worcestershire sauce

3 tablespoons tomato purée

1 teaspoon mild curry powder

1 tablespoon finely chopped shallots

1 garlic clove, crushed

1 tablespoon salted capers, rinsed, well drained and chopped

6 anchovy fillets in olive oil, drained and finely chopped

2 tablespoons chopped fresh parsley

1 teaspoon fresh thyme leaves

115 g unsalted butter, softened

a large, flameproof roasting tin

Serves 4

To make the café de Paris butter, put all of the ingredients in a food processor and process until well combined. Lay a piece of clingfilm on a work surface. Spoon the butter down the centre, then roll up firmly to make a log. The butter can be made 1–2 days in advance and refrigerated until needed. It should be removed from the refrigerator 1 hour before you plan to serve the beef. It can also be frozen for up to 1 month and defrosted before use.

Remove the beef from the refrigerator 1 hour before cooking and rub it all over with the salt and pepper.

Preheat the oven to 220°C (425°F) Gas 7.

Set the roasting tin over high heat. Add the oil to the pan and heat until very hot. Add the beef and cook for 4 minutes, turning every minute, until it is well browned all over. Transfer the roasting tin to the preheated oven and cook for 10 minutes. Turn the beef over and cook for a further 5 minutes. Remove the beef from the oven and sit it on a large sheet of foil. Pour over any pan juices and lightly wrap up in the foil. Let rest in a warm place for 15–20 minutes.

Bring a saucepan of lightly salted water to the boil. Add the asparagus and cook for 1 minute. Drain well. Heat the butter in a frying pan set over high heat. Add the asparagus, season well with salt and pepper and stir-fry for 3–4 minutes, until just wilting and lightly golden.

To serve, plate thick slices of the beef and put a few slices of café de Paris butter on top. Arrange the asparagus alongside.

sweet things

messy strawberries Romanoff

This is a foolproof dessert that pays homage to a popular fine dining dessert from the 1970s. Shop-bought meringues are roughly broken and arranged on a serving platter, then topped with whipped cream and Cointreau-macerated ripe summer strawberries.

500 g fresh strawberries, hulled

65 ml Cointreau or other orange-flavoured liqueur

6 shop-bought meringues

125 ml single or whipping cream

4 tablespoons icing sugar, plus extra for dusting

Serves 4

Put the strawberries in a non-reactive bowl and add the Cointreau. Cover and let sit at room temperature for 3 hours, stirring often.

Roughly break each meringue into 3–4 pieces and put them on a serving platter.

Put the cream in a grease-free bowl and use a hand-held electrc whisk to whip. Add the icing sugar, a little at a time, as you whip until the mixture forms soft peaks.

Spoon the cream over the meringue pieces then arrange the strawberries on top, along with a tablespoon or two of the macerating juice. Dust liberally with icing sugar just before serving.

Next time: Try replacing the strawberries with raspberries or blackberries or even sliced poached peaches, scattered with toasted flaked almonds.

fresh raspberry and almond tart

This tart tastes better the day after it's made, which makes it ideal for preparing ahead of time.

150 g fresh raspberries, frozen until firm

1 egg

3 tablespoons caster sugar

1 tablespoon plain flour

75 g unsalted butter

chilled cream, to serve (optional)

almond shortcrust pastry:

50 g ground almonds

200 g plain flour

80 g caster sugar

125 g unsalted butter, chilled and cubed

a rectangular tart tin, 37 x 10 cm, lightly greased

Serves 6–8

Preheat the oven to 180°C (350°F) Gas 4.

To make the pastry, put the ground almonds, flour and sugar in a food processor. With the motor running, add a cube of butter at a time until it is all incorporated and the mixture resembles coarse breadcrumbs. Add 2 tablespoons cold water and process until just combined. Be careful not to overprocess.

Tip the pastry out onto a lightly-floured work surface and knead to form a ball. Roll it out between 2 layers of baking paper until it is about 5 cm longer and 5 cm wider than the tart tin. Carefully lift the pastry into the tin and use your fingers to press it down into the base and sides, letting it overhang. Prick the base all over with a fork and bake in the preheated oven for 20 minutes, until lightly golden. Break off the overhanging pastry.

Put the egg, sugar and flour in a bowl and use a balloon whisk to beat until thick and pale. Put the butter in a small saucepan and set over medium heat. Let melt until frothy and dark golden with a nutty aroma. Working quickly, pour the melted butter over the egg mixture and beat well. Scatter the raspberries in the tart case. Pour the warm batter over the raspberries. Bake in the still-hot oven for about 45 minutes, until the top resembles a golden meringue. Let cool for 30 minutes before serving. Cut into slices and serve with chilled cream, if liked.

See photograph on page 134.

pear, almond and mascarpone tart

This recipe works best if the pears are on the overripe side so that they are fork-tender when cooked.

4 very ripe pears
1 tablespoon freshly squeezed lemon juice
4 tablespoons caster sugar
125 g mascarpone
1 egg
1 tablespoon plain flour
100 g flaked almonds
2 tablespoons granulated sugar
chilled cream or vanilla ice cream, to serve

pastry:
200 g plain flour
4 tablespoons caster sugar
80 g unsalted butter, chilled and cubed

a loose-bottomed tart tin, 24 cm diameter, lightly greased and floured

Serves 8–10

To make the pastry, put the flour and sugar in a food processor and pulse to combine. With the motor running, add the butter and 1–2 tablespoons cold water and mix until the mixture resembles coarse breadcrumbs and starts to gather in lumps. Transfer to a lightly-floured work surface and briefly knead to form a ball. Wrap in clingfilm and chill for 1 hour, until firm.

Preheat the oven to 180°C (350°F) Gas 4.

Coarsely grate the chilled pastry into a large bowl. Using lightly floured hands, scatter the grated pastry into the prepared tart tin and use your fingers to gently press it in until the entire base and the side of the tin are covered. Bake in the preheated oven for about 25 minutes, until lightly golden. Let cool.

Peel, halve and core the pears. Put them in a non-reactive bowl with the lemon juice and 1 tablespoon of the caster sugar. Put the remaining caster sugar in a food processor. Add the mascarpone, egg and flour and process to form a thick paste. Spread the mixture over the pastry. Arrange the pears on top and scatter with the almonds and granulated sugar. Bake in the still-hot oven for 40–45 minutes, until the pears are soft and the mascarpone mixture has set. Serve in slices with cream or vanilla ice cream on the side.

See photograph on page 135.

affogato parfait

An affogato is a fantastic Italian dessert – a scoop of vanilla ice cream is doused in a shot of hot espresso coffee and sometimes a sweet Italian liqueur such as Frangelico, Amaretto or Strega. Here we have all the flavours of an affogato in a parfait log. You can make it well in advance, then simply remove it from the freezer, sprinkle with nuts, slice and serve. I like to serve it with a little glass of liqueur on the side.

125 ml strong black espresso coffee
125 g caster sugar
1 vanilla pod
5 egg yolks
3 tablespoons Frangelico (Italian hazelnut liqueur) or grappa
500 g crème fraîche
250 ml double cream
100 g hazelnuts, lightly toasted and roughly chopped

a loaf tin, 8 x 22 cm, lined with clingfilm

Serves 6–8

Put the coffee and sugar in a small saucepan and set over high heat. Rub the vanilla pod between your palms to soften it, then use a sharp knife to split it open lengthways. Scrape the seeds directly into the saucepan. Bring the mixture to the boil, then reduce the heat to medium and let the liquid simmer for 10 minutes, stirring occassionally, until syrupy. Remove from the heat.

Put the egg yolks in a large bowl and use a balloon whisk to beat until thick and pale. Add the warm coffee syrup. Beat until well combined, then add the Frangelico. Add the crème fraîche and cream and beat until well combined. Pour into the prepared loaf tin and freeze overnight.

Remove the parfait from the freezer and let it sit for a few minutes before carefully turning out onto a chilled serving platter. Sprinkle with the hazelnuts and slice into individual portions to serve.

Next time: For an almond-flavoured version, use Amaretto di Saronno instead of Frangelico and sprinkle the parfait with toasted flaked almonds or crushed amaretti biscuits.

summer fruit compote with zabaglione

Zabaglione is another classic Italian dessert that combines a few simple ingredients to stunning effect. It needs to be made at the very last minute, so it will keep you in the kitchen for a short while, but it is well worth the effort. I have used strawberries, peaches and nectarines here, as they taste and look so good together, but any combination of your favourite summer fruits will work. I like to serve small glasses of floral dessert wine alongside this.

220 g white granulated sugar

2 nectarines, stoned and cut into thick wedges

2 peaches, stoned and cut into thick wedges

500 g fresh strawberries, hulled

zabaglione:

4 egg yolks

60 g caster sugar

100 ml Marsala or sweet sherry

Serves 4–6

Put the granulated sugar in a large saucepan with 750 ml water and set over high heat. Bring to the boil and boil for 5 minutes. Remove from the heat and let cool completely.

Put the fruit in a non-reactive bowl and pour the cooled syrup over the top. Cover and chill for 3–6 hours.

To make the zabaglione, put the egg yolks, caster sugar and Marsala in a large heatproof bowl. Set the bowl over a saucepan of barely simmering water, making sure the bottom of the bowl does not come into contact with the water.

Use a balloon whisk or hand-held electric whisk to beat gently for a few minutes, until well combined, then beat more vigorously for about 8–10 minutes, until the mixture has doubled in volume and is thick and spoonable.

Use a slotted spoon to transfer the fruit to a serving platter and spoon the warm zabaglione over the top. Serve immediately.

roasted hazelnut and chocolate cake

There are very few ingredients in this fantastic recipe, so do use really good-quality chocolate, not only for flavour but also because the content of cocoa fat solids will influence the result. It has a very soft texture, so it's important to let it cool before slicing.

1½ tablespoons cocoa powder

100 g raw hazelnuts

125 g dark chocolate (minimum 70% cocoa solids), roughly broken into pieces

1 tablespoon strong black espresso coffee

1 tablespoon brandy

100 g caster sugar

100 g butter

3 eggs, separated

a springform cake tin, 23 cm diameter, greased and lined

Serves 8–10

Preheat the oven to 170ºC (325ºF) Gas 3.

Sprinkle the cocoa powder into the cake tin and gently tap the side and bottom of the tin until evenly coated.

Spread the hazelnuts out on a baking tray and roast in the preheated oven for 10 minutes, shaking the tray after 5 minutes, until the skins are dark. Remove from the oven and let cool completely. Wrap the hazelnuts in a clean tea towel and use the towel to rub the nuts vigorously, to remove as much skin as possible. Pick any remaining skin off the nuts and put them in a food processor. Process until very finely chopped. Set aside.

Put the chocolate, coffee and brandy in a heatproof bowl. Set the bowl over a saucepan of barely simmering water, making sure the bottom of the bowl does not come into contact with the water. Let the chocolate melt, then remove from the heat and stir until smooth. Add the sugar, butter and egg yolks to the chocolate mixture in the warm bowl and beat until smooth. Transfer the mixture into a mixing bowl and fold in the roasted hazelnuts.

Put the egg whites in a clean, grease-free bowl and beat until stiff peaks form. Fold the egg whites into the chocolate mixture in two batches. Spoon the mixture into the prepared cake tin and bake in the still-hot oven for 20 minutes, until slightly risen yet still a little wobbly in the centre. Let cool to room temperature before serving.

See photographs on pages 140–141.

chocolate marquise

If you are a fan of real chocolate mousse you will love this. It is rich with butter and cream but unlike mousse, does not involve egg whites, so is heavier with a velvety texture. The great thing about it from an entertaining point of view is that there is no baking, as it sets into a loaf tin and can be left to chill in the refrigerator until you are ready to serve.

3 egg yolks

115 g caster sugar

200 g dark chocolate (minimum 70% cocoa solids), roughly broken into pieces

75 g unsalted butter, at room temperature

2 tablespoons cocoa powder

125 ml single cream

125 ml crème fraîche

2 small sweet oranges

1 small punnet blackberries, to serve

a loaf tin, 8 x 22 cm, lined with clingfilm

Serves 6–8

Put the egg yolks and sugar in a heatproof bowl and use a hand-held electric whisk to beat for 5 minutes, until pale and thick. Set the bowl over a saucepan of barely simmering water, making sure the bottom of the bowl does not come into contact with the water. Add the chocolate and stir as it melts. Add 1 tablespoon of the butter at a time and beat until well combined. Remove the bowl from the heat and gently fold in the cocoa powder. Let cool for about 10 minutes.

Put the cream and crème fraîche in a separate bowl and gently beat until soft peaks form. Fold about 65 ml of the cream mixture into the chocolate mixture, then add the remaining cream mixture. Spoon into the prepared loaf tin, cover and refrigerate overnight.

Peel the oranges, removing all the white pith, and slice them thinly. Pick over the blackberries and wash if necessary.

Remove the marquise from the refrigerator and carefully turn out onto a chilled serving platter. Cut into thick slices and serve with the orange slices and blackberries arranged on the side.

white chocolate pots

This is a simple yet indulgent treat that uses just three ingredients. It's very rich indeed, so just a small portion is all that's needed to satisfy even the most sweet-toothed of guests.

100 g good-quality white chocolate, broken into pieces
½ vanilla pod
200 ml double cream
a selection of fresh summer berries, to serve (optional)

6 small individual serving bowls, such as ramekins or coffee cups

Serves 4–6

Put the chocolate in a heatproof bowl.

Rub the vanilla pod between your palms to soften it then use a sharp knife to split it open lengthways. Scrape the seeds directly into the bowl with the chocolate.

Set the bowl over a saucepan of barely simmering water, making sure the bottom of the bowl does not come into contact with the water. Let the chocolate slowly melt then remove the bowl from the heat and stir the chocolate until smooth.

Put the cream in a bowl and whisk until thick and soft peaks form. Fold the cream into the melted chocolate.

Spoon the mixture into individual serving dishes and refrigerate for at least 6 hours before serving. Serve on its own or with summer berries, if liked.

chocolate truffles

These elegant cocoa-dusted truffles are a cinch to make and perfect for those guests who are in denial about wanting a 'real' dessert. Serve them with coffee, balancing one on the saucer of the cup, or arrange them on a plate and see how long they last.

200 g dark chocolate (minimum 70% cocoa solids), broken into pieces
5 tablespoons single cream
125 g butter, softened
2 teaspoons Grand Marnier or other flavoured liqueur (optional)
3 tablespoons cocoa powder, sifted

a melon baller

Makes about 36

Put the chocolate, cream and butter in a heatproof bowl. Set the bowl over a saucepan of barely simmering water, making sure the bottom of the bowl does not come into contact with the water. Let the chocolate and butter melt, stirring often, until glossy.

Remove from the heat and stir in the Grand Marnier. Transfer to a clean, non-reactive dish and refrigerate for 3 hours, until firm.

Chill 2 large plates. Sprinkle the cocoa powder onto one of the plates. Dip a melon baller into warm water and use it to scoop out a small ball of the chocolate mixture. Put it on the plate with the cocoa and roll the ball around until evenly coated in cocoa. Transfer the ball to the second chilled plate and repeat to make about 36 truffles. Keep refrigerated until ready to serve. The truffles will keep for up to 1 week if refrigerated in an airtight container.

cherry and walnut brownies

The fruit and nut combination in these brownies gives them a rather Christmassy feel – you could go the whole way and substitute glacé cherries for the fresh if you like. A rich, dense and gooey chocolate brownie is always a crowd pleaser and a very mature way to end a meal!

350 g caster sugar

80 g cocoa powder

60 g plain flour

1 teaspoon baking powder

4 eggs, beaten

200 g dark chocolate (minimum 70% cocoa solids), broken into small pieces

100 g fresh cherries, stoned and halved

200 g walnut halves

250 g unsalted butter, melted

cream or vanilla ice cream, to serve (optional)

a cake tin, 20 cm square, greased and lined with baking paper

Serves 10–12

Preheat the oven to 170°C (325°F) Gas 3.

Put the sugar in a large bowl. Sift in the cocoa powder, flour and baking powder.

Add the eggs and mix until just combined. Stir in the chocolate pieces, cherries and walnuts. Put the butter in a small saucepan and set over very low heat to melt. Pour the melted butter into the chocolate mixture and stir in, but without overmixing.

Spoon the mixture into the prepared tin and bake in the preheated oven for 45 minutes. Let cool for at least 30 minutes before cutting into squares. Serve with chilled cream or vanilla ice cream, if liked.

blueberry madeleines with lemon cream

A favourite in the pâtisseries of France, delicate madeleine cakes are traditionally baked in a tin with shell-shaped holes. I've given them a new twist here by adding blueberries. The lemon cream is really a 'posset' – a traditional English dessert that uses the natural citric acid present in lemons to set the cream. It is smooth and velvety, almost butter-like, and offers a nice contrast in texture to the golden sponge cakes.

2 eggs

65 g raw caster sugar

100 g plain flour

75 g unsalted butter, melted and cooled

50 g fresh blueberries, frozen until firm

icing sugar, for dusting

lemon cream:
125 ml single cream

125 ml double cream

65 g caster sugar

2 tablespoons freshly squeezed lemon juice

6 small wine or liqueur glasses

a 12-hole madeleine tin, greased and lightly dusted with flour

Serves 6

To make the lemon cream, put both the creams in a saucepan and add the caster sugar. Set over medium heat and cook, stirring often, until the mixture starts to boil around the edge. Reduce the heat to medium/low and let the cream gently bubble for about 3 minutes. Remove from the heat and stir in the lemon juice. Let sit for 10 minutes. Stir just once and pour the mixture into the serving glasses. Refrigerate for at least 6 hours, until set.

Preheat the oven to 200°C (400°F) Gas 6.

Put the eggs and raw caster sugar in a bowl and use a hand-held whisk to beat for about 5 minutes, until pale and thick. Sift in the flour and add the butter and blueberries. Spoon the mixture into the prepared tin and bake in the preheated oven for 12–15 minutes, until the cakes are golden and spring back when gently pressed in the centre. Let the cakes cool and dust liberally with icing sugar. Serve 2 cakes per person with a glass of lemon cream.

See photographs on pages 148–149.

Moroccan apple pie

The method of using layers of buttered filo pastry and inverting the pie was inspired by Moroccan 'bastilla', but here the filling is vanilla-infused apples.

6 tart green apples, peeled, cored and thinly sliced

1 teaspoon finely grated lemon zest

2 tablespoons freshly squeezed lemon juice

1 vanilla pod

115 g caster sugar

1 teaspoon ground cinnamon

1 teaspoon cornflour

80 g unsalted butter, melted and cooled

8 sheets of filo pastry, defrosted if frozen

icing sugar, for dusting

a springform cake tin, 22 cm diameter, lined with baking paper

Serves 8–10

Put the apples in a non-reactive bowl with the lemon zest and juice. Rub the vanilla pod between your palms to soften it, then use a sharp knife to split it open lengthways. Scrape the seeds into the bowl with the apples. Add half of the caster sugar and toss to coat. Put the remaining caster sugar in a small bowl with the cinnamon and mix to combine. Set aside.

Put the apples in a saucepan with 2 tablespoons water and set over medium heat. Cover and cook for 10 minutes, stirring occasionally, until the apples are soft but not mushy. Transfer the apples to a bowl and let cool. When completely cool, stir in the cornflour.

Preheat the oven to 220°C (425°F) Gas 7. Put a baking tray in the oven to heat. Brush the cake tin with a little of the melted butter.

Lay a sheet of filo on a clean work surface and lightly brush with melted butter. Sprinkle over some of the cinnamon sugar. Repeat using 3 more sheets of filo. Lift the filo into the cake tin. Gently press it into the tin, letting the ends hang over the rim. Repeat with the remaining filo, but lay the second stack across the first one so that the entire rim of the tin is draped in pastry. Spoon the apples into the tin and use the back of a spoon to gently press them down. Fold the ends of the filo towards the centre of the tin to enclose the filling. Lightly brush with melted butter.

Working quickly, remove the hot baking tray from the oven and line with baking paper. Carefully invert the tin onto the tray. Remove the side and base of the tin and brush the top of the pie with melted butter. Bake in the preheated oven for 30–35 minutes, until golden and crisp. Dust liberally with icing sugar and serve warm.

baked cheesecake

Who doesn't love a good baked cheesecake? Make this the day before you want to serve it and don't stress about cracks in the surface – they add character! For the best result, bring the cream cheese, eggs and sour cream to room temperature before using.

160 g very dry, slightly sweet biscuits, such as Rich Tea or Arnott's Coffee Biscuits

225 g caster sugar

100 g unsalted butter, melted

750 g full-fat cream cheese

5 eggs

300 ml sour cream

1 teaspoon finely grated lemon zest

a springform cake tin, 23 cm diameter base, lined with baking paper and lightly greased

Serves 8–10

Preheat the oven to 170°C (325°F) Gas 3. Wrap the entire outside of the prepared cake tin in 2 layers of foil.

Put the biscuits and 1 tablespoon of the sugar in a food processor and process to a fine crumb. Add the melted butter and process until well combined. Tip the crumb mixture into the prepared tin and spread evenly over the base. Use the bottom of a glass tumbler to firmly press the crumb mixture into the tin. Bake in the preheated oven for 20 minutes. Remove and let cool completely.

Put the cream cheese and remaining sugar in a bowl, preferably that of an electric mixer with a paddle attachment, and beat for 2 minutes, until smooth and well combined. Add the eggs, one at a time, beating well between each addition and scraping down the side of the mixer bowl. Add the lemon zest and sour cream. Beat until the mixture is lump-free.

Pour the mixture into the prepared tin and level the top with a pallette knife. Bake in the still-hot oven for 1 hour, until the top of the cheesecake is golden but the centre is still wobbly. Turn the oven off and partially open the oven door. Let the cheesecake cool in the oven for 1 hour. Refrigerate for 6 hours, or ideally overnight.

Remove the cheesecake from the refrigerator 1 hour before eating. When ready to serve, run a warm, dry knife around the edge of the cake and remove the springform side. Cut into generous wedges.

See photographs on page 152–153.

pan plum crumble

This comforting crumble is cooked under the grill and you can even serve it at the table straight out of the frying pan – it doesn't get any more casual than that! Plums are good, but you could use any fruit you fancy – just be aware that soft summer berries will need very little time in the pan, while apples and pears will require a little longer.

185 ml freshly squeezed orange juice
2 tablespoons caster sugar
6 ripe plums, halved and stoned
100 g self-raising flour
60 g soft brown sugar
60 g porridge oats
50 g unsalted butter, cubed and chilled
vanilla ice cream, to serve

Serves 4–6

Put the orange juice and caster sugar in a small frying pan and set it over high heat. Bring the mixture to the boil, then reduce the heat to medium. Add the plums, cut-side down, and cook for 5 minutes. Turn the plums over and cook for a further 5 minutes, until they have softened yet still retain their shape and the liquid has almost evaporated. Remove the pan from the heat and set aside.

Preheat the grill to medium.

Put the flour, brown sugar and oats in a bowl and mix just to combine. Add the butter and use your fingertips to rub it into the dry ingredients.

Sprinkle the mixture evenly over the plums and slide the frying pan under the hot grill for 2–3 minutes, until the crumble is golden. Serve warm with a scoop of vanilla ice cream.

spiced muscat figs

Muscat is a grape variety that produces deliciously sweet and syrupy dessert wines known as moscato in Italy and moscatel in Spain. Whichever one you choose, the result will be the same – a deliciously fragrant and light dessert that will wow your guests.

250 ml muscat (sweet dessert wine)
125 g caster sugar
1 vanilla pod
2 cardamom pods, lightly crushed
2 strips of orange zest
8 fresh green figs

Serves 4

Put the muscat, sugar, vanilla and cardamom pods and orange zest in a medium saucepan and set over high heat. Bring the mixture to the boil, then reduce the heat to medium. Add the figs to the pan, cover and cook for 20–25 minutes, until the figs are very tender. Remove the figs from the pan with a slotted spoon and set aside.

Return the liquid to the boil and cook for 8–10 minutes, until thick and syrupy.

Serve 2 figs per person, with the syrup spooned over the top.

See photographs on pages 156–157.

flan casero

This is basically a giant crème caramel, and as such is Spain's most popular dessert, where it is on every menu in every region. And rightly so, as the simple, yet delicious combination of rich, baked egg custard with a caramelized sugar syrup is a real winner – your guests will almost certainly want seconds.

450 g white granulated sugar
1 litre full-fat milk
2 teaspoons vanilla extract
10 eggs

Serves 10–12

Put half of the sugar in a large, heavy-based frying pan and set over medium heat. Cook until the sugar has dissolved and is just starting to turn golden around the sides of the pan. Increase the heat to high and gently swirl the pan over the heat so the sugar dissolves and is the colour of golden syrup or honey. Remove the pan from the heat before the sugar starts to burn and continue swirling the pan so that the side is covered in the caramel. Do this until the caramel starts to set. Set aside until needed.

Preheat the oven to 180°C (350°F) Gas 4 and put the frying pan with the caramel in a large roasting tin.

Put the milk and vanilla extract in a large saucepan and heat over medium heat until the milk reaches boiling point, but remove it from the heat just before it boils.

Put the eggs and remaining sugar in a bowl and whisk until well combined. Add the hot milk to the egg mixture and whisk to combine. Strain the mixture through a fine sieve, then pour the custard into the frying pan, over the caramel. Pour enough cold water into the roasting tin to come almost to the top of the frying pan and carefully put into the preheated oven.

Cook for 1¼ hours, until the custard has set. It may still be slightly wobbly in the centre. Lift the frying pan out of the roasting tin and let it sit at room temperature until cool. Refrigerate for 3 hours or ideally overnight.

To serve, run a knife around the side of the frying pan, to remove any stuck-on bits. Sit a serving plate, larger than the frying pan, over the top and quickly turn the flan out onto the plate. Sit it on a work surface and tap the bottom of the frying pan to release the flan. Use a large spoon to serve.

panna cotta with red wine syrup

The secret of a great panna cotta is in the wobble. I have eaten many different versions – some of them made from packet mixes – but this one is particularly good. Panna cotta literally means 'cooked cream' in Italian and is said to have originated from Lombardy, where the cream and milk are very rich, so it's important to use full-fat milk for a good result.

3 gelatine leaves
500 ml single cream
250 ml full-fat milk
125 g caster sugar
1 vanilla pod
50 g pistachios, roughly chopped

red wine syrup:
250 ml red wine
65 g caster sugar

6 individual moulds

Serves 6

Put the gelatine leaves in a bowl with enough cold water to cover and let soak for 5 minutes.

Put the cream, milk and sugar in a small saucepan. Rub the vanilla pod between your palms to soften it, then use a sharp knife to split it open lengthways. Scrape the seeds into the pan. Set the mixture over low heat and cook, stirring, until the sugar has dissolved. Squeeze all of the liquid from the gelatine leaves and add them to the pan. Stir until the gelatine has completely dissolved. Pour the mixture into individual moulds and refrigerate for at least 6 hours, preferably overnight, until set.

To make the red wine syrup, put the wine and sugar in a small saucepan and set over high heat. Bring to the boil and cook for 7–8 minutes, stirring constantly, until the mixture is syrupy. It will thicken as it cools. Let cool.

To serve, turn the moulds upside down on a serving plate. Rub a warm cloth on the outside of each mould to soften the set gelatine and the panna cotta should separate from the mould and drop out onto the plate.

Drizzle the red wine syrup around the panna cotta and sprinkle the pistachios over the top to serve.

index